1. For the Love of Wisdom

FOR THE LOVE OF WISDOM

"I will not call it my philosophy; for I did not make it.
God and humanity made it; and it made me."

Gilbert Keith Chesterton, Orthodoxy

For the Love of Wisdom

An Explanation of the Meaning and Purpose of Philosophy

CHRIS JOHN-TERRY

ALBA · HOUSE NEW · YORK

SOCIETY OF ST. PAUL, 2187 VICTORY BLVD., STATEN ISLAND, NY 10314

Library of Congress Cataloging-in-Publication Data

John-Terry, Chris.
     For the love of wisdom: an explanation of the meaning and purpose
of philosophy / Chris John-Terry.
          p.   cm.
     Includes bibliographical references.
     ISBN 0-8189-0695-2
     1. Philosophy — Introductions. 2. Catholic Church and philosophy.
I. Title.
B103.J64   1994
100 — dc20   94-13663
                                                    CIP

Produced and designed in the United States of America by the
Fathers and Brothers of the Society of St. Paul,
2187 Victory Boulevard, Staten Island, New York 10314,
as part of their communications apostolate.

ISBN: 0-8189-0695-2

© Copyright 1994 by the Society of St. Paul

Printing Information:

Current Printing - first digit	1	2	3	4	5	6	7	8	9	10

Year of Current Printing - first year shown

1994	1995	1996	1997	1998	1999

Contents

Foreword vii

Chapter 1: What is Philosophy? 1

   Philosophy as Science 3
   Philosophy as Universal Science 5
   Philosophy and Theology 7
   Philosophy and the Experimental Sciences 13
   The Method of Philosophy 16

Chapter 2: Challenges to Philosophy 21

   The Scandal of Philosophy 21
   Philosophy and Linguistic Analysis 23
   Philosophy and Empiricism 25
   Philosophy and Logical Positivism 27
   Bertrand Russell's Attack 30

Chapter 3: The Goal of Philosophy 33

   The Value of Philosophy 36
   The Philosopher in Society 39

Chapter 4: The Marks of an Authentic Philosophy 41

   Philosophy Begins in Wonder 41
   Philosophy is Dialectical 44

Philosophy is Clear 51
Philosophy is Perennial 52
Philosophy is Open to Divine Revelation 57

Chapter 5: Saint Thomas and Philosophy 63
The Language of Thomistic Philosophy 65
The Branches of Philosophy in the Tradition
    of Saint Thomas 68

Chapter 6: The Future of Philosophy 75
The Future of Philosophy 78

Foreword

The purpose of this book is to preserve a treasure. For centuries philosophers have labored to find out the truth about themselves, the universe and God. The fruit of this long tradition of intellectual pursuit, now known as the *philosophia perennis*, is a legacy that the finest minds in history have left to humankind.

We, however, are in danger of losing this precious heritage. Dazzled by the success of the physical and the experimental sciences, many scholars still regard *experience* and *experiment* as the only legitimate sources of certainty and knowledge. For them, only truths about the observable world are worth seeking, while philosophical discourses on non-sensible entities, such as "God" or the "soul," are futile. They say that metaphysical statements are unreliable because they are not, even in principle, verifiable by the methods of modern science.

Preoccupied with what psychologists aptly called the "rat race" and others call "progress," most people have also abandoned the pursuit of wisdom altogether. They do not regard any knowledge as worthwhile unless it affords some economic advantage, or unless it leads to more pleasure, honor or fame.

Not only is the pursuit of wisdom neglected nowadays, but it is also in danger of being replaced by false substitutes. On the one hand there are scientistic thinkers and rationalists who glorify Science and Reason as substitutes for Wisdom and Faith. On the other hand there are idealists and irrationalists who either deny the reality of a world independent of the mind or the mind's ability to know a world outside it. We also observe the growing influence in our culture of eastern religious thought that equates wisdom with *occult* knowledge. The proponents of this world-view are neither rationalists nor irrationalists. Still, they pose a threat to what Boethius called "Dame Philosophy," for philosophy aims at a clear and reasoned knowledge of natural facts, not at nebulous speculations about the supernatural.

The present work aims to explain the true meaning and purpose of our philosophical heritage. It will show the *difference* between wisdom and its counterfeits.

Philosophical truths comprise not only the truths attained by the Greeks, but also those that philosophers have rationally established under the influence of Christianity. "Christian philosophy," as Pope Leo XIII called it, was largely the achievement of medieval theologians. Therefore, its recognition by the present, technological world as a competing and relevant branch of knowledge is difficult to obtain. To win the respect of contemporary scholars, Maurice De Wulf and the "modern scholastics" proposed a philosophy that pretends to labor independently of the Christian faith. But it is not necessary to do this. Nor is it beneficial to deny philosophy's indebtedness to Christianity. Even poetry and the arts have benefited from the influence of the Christian religion. Neither Dante nor Shakespeare, nor Giotto nor Michelangelo would be understandable without a knowledge of Christian theology. Similarly, modern philosophy could not have been what it was, if there had been no Christian religion. The writings of modern philosophers — Nicolas Malebranche, Baruch Spinoza, David Hume, Immanuel Kant and even Karl Marx — all betray the profound influence of Christianity in their thoughts. Therefore, it is not necessary to divorce philosophy from Christianity just to be respectable. Besides being untrue to its historical roots, the deliberate denial of Christian influence in the work of reason retards philosophy's growth and unnecessarily exposes the human mind to the pitfalls of reason. As the eminent historian of philosophy, Etienne Gilson, noted, the errors of Greek philosophy are precisely the errors into which a philosophy, unaided by Christian revelation, falls.

Therefore, this book is different from many contemporary books on the subject. Here the author makes his reflections on the meaning of philosophy, unembarrassed by the fact that he is doing it from the standpoint of a Christian philosopher. This procedure might seem archaic. However, we can no longer disregard the guidance that revealed truth offers to an intellectual enterprise that is struggling against the powerful currents of scientism, irrationalism and despair. Of course, we must always keep the formal distinction between philosophy and theology. But philosophy today cannot survive *as* philosophy unless it is Christian philosophy.

May this book help us to understand more and to judge better. May it remind us of the superiority of Wisdom over Science and of our need to continue the search for truth while seeking our livelihood. May it develop in each of us a certain reverence for disinterested knowledge and an appreciation of truth as the basis of justice, peace and human fellowship. Finally, may we learn to love and to cherish the wisdom of the Masters and, if possible, to continue the great tradition that has brought us this valuable inheritance.

FOR THE LOVE OF WISDOM

Chapter One

What is Philosophy?

Many ancient civilizations had a conception of the world and of man that might be called "philosophical." However, ancient speculations were for the most part so mixed with mythology and religious beliefs that, except in Greece, philosophy did not develop as a respectable science until the 6th century B.C. The pioneers of Greek science — among them Thales, Anaximander and Anaximenes — were also the first philosophers. They were profoundly interested in discovering the ultimate constitution and nature of the universe, but they differed from other ancient thinkers in their approach. They wanted an *objective, rational and natural*, as opposed to a subjective, poetic and mythical *account of natural facts*.

Pythagoras invented the word "philosophy." The word came from the Greek *philia*, which means love, and *sophias*, which means wisdom. Therefore, philosophy literally means "the love of wisdom." According to an ancient tradition, Pythagoras thought that no man could possess wisdom, which is a most comprehensive and profound knowledge of things. Wisdom was the privileged possession only of God. Therefore, he said, no man could justly call himself "wise." At best he could only call himself a "lover" or "seeker" of wisdom, that is, a philosopher.

Heraclitus was among the first philosophers of Greece. He

1

thought that wisdom did not consist in knowing a multitude of facts, but in having a unified view of reality. However, Heraclitus merely handed out his thoughts as revelations of the *Logos* (the World-Soul). In contrast, his rival Parmenides constantly tried to prove the opposite views. It was from him that philosophy gained its reputation as "a severe discipline of reasoned knowledge."

Plato went even further toward a better understanding of philosophy. For him, the true philosopher is the *dialectician*, the one who apprehends the essences of things. Plato thinks that the eternal essences of things, called "Ideas," exist in a higher grade of reality, while the finite, sensible objects around us are but imitations or "copies" of the eternal Ideas. So, Plato distinguished the true philosopher from the "the lovers of sounds and sights," the *sophists* who concentrate merely on sensible things and their appearances. Unlike the true philosopher, the sophist (counterfeit philosopher) takes appearances for reality and "puts the copy in the place of the real object."[1]

Aristotle, Plato's distinguished student, accepted Plato's concept that true wisdom consists in a genuine knowledge of things. However, he added that since the wise man differed from other people by his knowledge of first principles, so philosophy, as wisdom, should be the science that seeks the first causes of things. Following Aristotle, Saint Thomas further distinguished philosophy from theology, saying that the difference between them is that between natural and revealed wisdom. Accordingly, the followers of Aristotle and Saint Thomas now define philosophy as *the science of things by their first causes, to the extent that it is attainable by the natural light of reason.*

Although the above definition has been challenged recently, we shall show in the next chapter that it is still an excellent, if not

---

[1] Plato, *The Republic*, Book V, Tr. by Benjamin Jowett in Vol. 7 of *Great Books* (Encyclopædia Britannica, Inc. 1952), p. 371.

the best, definition of philosophy to date. In this chapter we shall only explain the elements of this definition.

PHILOSOPHY AS SCIENCE

Philosophy is a science. However, it is not a science in the corrupt sense that restricts the denotation of the word to physics, chemistry and the other experimental sciences. Rather, it is a science in its original signification as *certa cognitio per causas*, which means "a knowledge of things attained by an investigation of their causes." Let us explain what this means.

Saying that philosophy is a science means that it is a branch of knowledge. Indeed, the word "science" came from the Latin verb *scire*, which means "to know." However, science is not just any sort of knowledge. A man truly has the science of a thing only if he has a knowledge of its causes. For the mere knowledge that fire is hot, or that fire burns, is not science. But knowing *why* fire is hot, or knowing the *causes* that make fire burn, is science. Without a knowledge of its causes, we only know the fact, but not the reasons for the fact. We merely have knowledge, but not science.

When someone is sick, we do not call just any man. Instead we call a doctor. Now, the word "doctor" comes from the Latin word *doctus*, which means a learned person. To treat a sick person, we do not want to call just any man, but a doctor of medicine. Unlike the quack, the real doctor is a man of science. He has a knowledge of the *causes* that make people sick and the *causes* that would make them well again.

It is also by his knowledge of causes that we distinguish the man of experience from the man of science. The man of experience, or the "practical man," merely knows that certain things work. But the man of science also has an understanding of the reasons *why* they work. The man of science has a knowledge of facts *and* their causes. He has a knowledge of the *whys* of things.

This is why the man of science can teach, whereas the merely practical man cannot.[2]

Certitude is the natural result of knowing the causes of things. We are uncertain only as long as we do not know the causes of things or events. Certitude comes when we do not merely know the facts but also their causes. Now, since scientific knowledge is a knowledge of causes, scientific knowledge must be a *certain* knowledge. Scientific knowledge is not merely opinion, conjecture or belief, but a certain knowledge that results from an analysis of causes.

In saying that scientific knowledge is certain, we do not mean to say that all the conclusions of science, including those obtained in the early stages of its development, possess absolute certitude. All that we mean is that certitude, and not merely probable opinion, is the ideal that it seeks to attain. For example, everyone agrees that physics is a science, yet we find plenty of theories and opinions in physics that are not certain, but only probable. In spite of this, we still regard physics as a science because, unlike the ancient mythologies, physics aims at certitude and not merely at probable opinion or belief.

Therefore, it is not necessary that an intellectual discipline first possess absolute certitude before it could justly be called a science. Indeed, no human science that is still developing could contain nothing but certain conclusions. The definition of science as *certa cognitio per causas* strictly applies only to science in its perfect stage.

Now, philosophy also is a science in this sense. It is a knowledge of things together with their causes. Philosophy does not merely gather facts, but also works to know the causes and reasons behind the facts. It does not merely make conjectures or opinions, but strives to know the *whys* and *wherefores* of things.

---

[2] Aristotle, *Metaphysics*, Bk. I, Ch. 1, 981b 5-10.

Therefore, philosophy is a science because it is a knowledge that, when brought to its perfection, results in certitude.

Like other human sciences, however, philosophy is still in a process of development. It has not yet reached its perfection or final stage. Although today there are elements in it that are certain, there are also many philosophical conclusions that are, strictly speaking, only opinions or probable conclusions. For example, Aristotle's conclusion, that *whatever is moved, is moved by another*, is metaphysically certain. But Saint Thomas' opinion, that the human soul begins to exist a few weeks after conception, is only a probable conclusion.

It was the mistake of older manuals on scholastic philosophy to give the impression that philosophy contained nothing but certain and incorrigible conclusions. Any conclusion of philosophy that is based on *axioms* or *self-evident principles* is, of course, certain. But the first principles of philosophy do not consist only of self-evident principles, such as the principle of non-contradiction, the principle of excluded middle, the principle of sufficient reason, etc. There are also some that are just plausible principles *derived from common experience*. Explanations based on these principles result only in probable opinions or *theories*. For example, Aristotle's hylemorphic doctrine is a philosophical *theory* that attempts to explain the essential mutability of bodily substances. It is based on the commonly observed fact of change.[3]

---

[3] Aristotle observes that in every thing that changes, the subject aquires a new characteristic while it loses an old one. For example, when an apple changes its color, the apple (the subject) acquires a new color while it loses its former color. However, Aristotle observes that bodies do not merely suffer superficial changes, such as changes in color or weight. Bodily substances can also be *substantially* changed, as when wood burns into ashes. So, Aristotle *theorized* that within the essence of every bodily being there must be an indeterminate but determinable subject of change, called *matter*, and a determining principle, called the *substantial form*. When a body changes substantially, its matter simply acquires a new substantial form while it loses the old one.

PHILOSOPHY AS UNIVERSAL SCIENCE

Philosophy is a science of *things*, that is, of real beings and not of mere abstractions. Many people think that philosophy deals merely with abstractions or speculations that have no bearing on reality. At the mention of the word "philosopher" they imagine a man sitting on a chair (like Rodin's statue of *The Thinker*), absorbed in deep thought, and completely unaware of the world around him. The contrary is true. Philosophy deals with concrete beings, and philosophers seek to understand the ultimate structure of reality. Of course, philosophy also uses concepts that are abstract, but so do the other sciences of reality, such as mathematical physics. Often, we have to make use of abstract concepts to understand concrete facts.

Philosophy is a science of things. More precisely, it is a science of *contingent beings*, that means, of real beings that are not self-existent. If beings that are not self-existent exist, then their existence demands an explanation. This is precisely what the philosopher seeks: the *causes* of, or the *reasons* for, the actual existence of things that need not be. The central problem of metaphysics (otherwise known as *first philosophy*) is the problem of *being*. For the philosopher's concern is not merely the question of *essence*, or *what* things are, but also and primarily the question of existence, or *why* they are.[4]

In Aristotle's definition, philosophy is the science, not merely of *some*, but of *all* contingent beings. Since everything but God is contingent, then both the whole material world and the world of spiritual creatures fall under the broad range of philosophy. For this reason, many scholars regard philosophy as a *universal* science.

---

[4] Since certainty results from a knowledge of causes, one must ask *what* a thing is and *why* it exists, to complete his knowledge of any object. The first question, *What is it?* may be answered by giving the object's intrinsic causes (material and formal cause), while the second question, *Why it exists?* may be answered by giving the object's extrinsic causes (efficient and final cause).

For example, William James describes philosophy as covering "the principles of explanation that underlie all things without exception, the elements common to gods and men and animals and stones, the first *whence* and the last *whither* of the whole cosmic procession, the conditions of all knowing, and the most general rules of human action."[5]

PHILOSOPHY AND THEOLOGY

Saying that philosophy deals with real, contingent beings does not mean that the consideration of God (who is a self-existent being) is altogether beyond the scope of philosophy. In fact, all major philosophers from ancient times to the present have displayed an absorbing interest in the question of God's existence, His nature and His action upon the world.

The principal subject-matter of philosophy is not God but contingent being. For we understand philosophy as the science of things *by their first causes*. Now, this does not make sense unless by "things" we mean *contingent beings*, for only contingent beings have causes. However, by reflecting on the fact that beings in the world have a beginning and an end, we discover their contingency and their need for a self-sufficient Being to explain their existence. So, the consideration of God becomes part of philosophical reflection, not on account of God, but on account of the whole contingent world. The so-called "philosophical proofs" for the existence of God are the result of an attempt to understand why the world exists, and not so much the result of an attempt to answer the question, "Is there a God?"

That part of philosophy which deals with God is *natural theology*, a subject that should be sharply distinguished from

---

[5] William James, *Some Problems of Philosophy* (New York: Longmans, Green & Co., 1911), p. 4.

revealed or *supernatural theology*. Revealed theology is a science that one attains, not by reason but by faith, and that derives its principles from divine revelation. Revealed theology treats of God as its principal subject-matter, and secondarily treats of contingent beings as His creatures. On the other hand, natural theology treats of contingent beings as its *principal* subject-matter, and secondarily treats of God as the First Principle or Cause of their actual existence. Saint Thomas Aquinas states this distinction very clearly:

> And so, theology or divine science is of two kinds. One, in which divine things are considered not as the subject of the science but as principles of the subject, is the kind of theology that the philosophers seek. The other, which considers these divine things themselves in their own right as the subject of a science, is the kind of theology that is handed down in sacred Scripture.[6]

The distinction between the philosophical science of God and supernatural theology is not an opposition. In fact, a certain harmony exists between reason and faith, a harmony that is nothing else than the harmony of truth with itself. It is the harmony of truth (as discovered by reason) with truth (as revealed by God). So, it is possible for a man to be a *philosopher* with respect to those truths that are accessible to reason, and a *believer* with respect to those truths that reason cannot attain without the aid of divine revelation.

Historically, the influence of divine revelation in the development of philosophical thought has been profound. It led to the birth of what Pope Leo XIII called "Christian philosophy,"[7] or the use of reason in scrutinizing the contents of divine revelation. During the Middle Ages Saint Anselm and Saint Thomas upheld the principle of *fides quaerens intellectum* — "faith seeking understanding" —

[6] Saint Thomas Aquinas, *Exposition of Boethius on the Trinity*, V, 4, c. Tr. by Vernon J. Bourke in *The Pocket Aquinas* (New York: Washington Square Press, 1969), p. 150.

[7] Pope Leo XIII, Encyclical Letter *Aeterni Patris*, 1879.

as expressing the beneficent effect of faith in the progress of human reason. The long treatises, which many philosophers from Descartes to Kant wrote about God, also show the positive contribution of Christianity in modern philosophical thought. This is hardly surprising. As Etienne Gilson said, "Once you are in possession of that revelation how can you possibly philosophize as though you had never heard of it?"[8]

Some say that there cannot be such a thing as a Christian philosophy any more than there can be such a thing as a Christian physics or a Christian mathematics. Some even say that the concept is a contradiction in terms, for Christianity is based on faith, whereas philosophy is based on reason. However, although there may not be such a thing as a Christian reason, there is such a thing as a Christian exercise of reason. Nothing prevents a philosopher from pursuing in a strictly rational manner the ultimate answers to the questions that arise from a knowledge of revealed data. Indeed, a philosophy that derives inspiration from the Sacred Scriptures in the questions that it raises, and that finds it to be an indispensable guide in the answers that it finds, is a *Christian philosophy*.[9]

For the believer, divine revelation is an indispensable ally of reason in two ways. First, it stimulates philosophical reflection on those matters that otherwise would remain unexplored in a purely natural quest of truth. For example, the theologian's attempt to defend the mystery of the Eucharist led to the philosophical knowledge that we now have of the nature of bodies. Because of its strictly supernatural character, the actual changing of the bread and wine into the Body and Blood of Christ (transubstantiation) cannot be proved. However, the Christian philosopher has succeeded on

---

[8] Etienne Gilson, *The Spirit of Medieval Philosophy* (New York: Charles Scribner's Sons, 1940), Chapter 1, p. 5. Tr. by A.H.C. Downes.

[9] In *The Spirit of Medieval Philosophy*, Chapter 2, p. 37, Etienne Gilson said, "Thus I call Christian, *every philosophy which, although keeping the two orders formally distinct, nevertheless considers the Christian revelation as an indispensable auxiliary to reason.*"

purely *rational* principles to discover what the nature of bodies must be if transubstantiation is to take place at all. This achievement is hardly possible without faith. Although the eucharistic presence is strictly incapable of proof, faith in this mystery inspired the Christian philosopher to refine his understanding of the nature and limitations of bodies. This is an instance where faith fecundates reason. We might say that divine revelation held the philosopher "by the hand" and set him, so to speak, in the right direction.[10]

Second, divine revelation offers an external check on the conclusions of philosophy. Since the source of both natural and supernatural truths is God, the Christian philosopher knows that no truth attained by reason can conflict with revealed truth. So, if a philosophical conclusion contradicts divine revelation, then it becomes doubtful and requires a review of the argument by which it was reached.[11] For example, Aristotle's arguments, which claim to prove that the universe always existed, contradict the revealed doctrine that the world had a beginning. Guided by his faith in the dogma of creation, Saint Thomas Aquinas reviewed Aristotle's arguments and showed that these arguments were not cogent. However, he did not do this by an appeal to faith, but by a correct and complete deduction of the consequences implied in the very same principles that Aristotle himself employed. Using strictly philosophical procedures, Saint Thomas showed that reason alone could neither prove nor disprove the eternity of the world. So, if the eternity of the world is not a rationally established fact, then the possibility arises that the world might have a beginning in time. That the world had a beginning may be impossible to prove, but now, at least, it is credible. Saint Thomas ended his analysis by saying that

---

[10] See Saint Thomas Aquinas, *The Disputed Questions on Truth* (Chicago: Henry Regnery Company, 1952), XIV, 10. Tr. by James V. McGlynn, S.J.

[11] Saint Thomas says, "If any point among the statements of the philosophers is found contrary to faith, this is not philosophy but rather an abuse of philosophy, resulting from a defect in reasoning." *Exposition of Boethius on the Trinity*, II, 3, c. Translated by Vernon J. Bourke in *The Pocket Aquinas*, p. 293.

the creation of the world by God in time was strictly an *article of faith*. This example illustrates what Christian philosophers through the ages have unanimously said about their philosophy. While it receives special insights and guidance from divine revelation, Christian philosophy bases its arguments on reason. So, it truly deserves the title of "philosophy."

Philosophy does not merely benefit from the knowledge of revealed data, but in return it also helps supernatural theology in a threefold way. First, philosophy aids in manifesting the truths of faith, not by proving revealed truths that are strictly undemonstrable, but by proving those truths about God that are attainable by reason — the so-called "preambles to the faith." In this manner, philosophy "paves the way" for faith. Second, philosophy manifests supernatural truths by showing their analogy to natural facts. For example, Saint Augustine explained the meaning of the Blessed Trinity by presenting many examples taken from philosophy. Third, philosophy helps theology by answering objections to the faith. Although above reason, revealed truths are not against reason. So, if there are any rational arguments that seem to discredit the contents of divine revelation, philosophy can show that these arguments lack the force of a true demonstration.

Although aided by philosophy, revealed theology is independent of philosophy. Supernatural theology does not borrow its principles from philosophy but derives them directly from God through revelation. As a higher wisdom, theology does not depend on philosophy as its superior, but merely uses it as its inferior. This explains Saint Thomas' famous conception of theology as Queen of the Sciences with philosophy as its "handmaid," *ancilla theologiae*.[12]

Although among the various sciences philosophy alone merits the name of *wisdom*, since it alone considers the highest causes, the

---

[12] Saint Thomas Aquinas, *Summa Theologica*, Part 1, Q. 1, Art. 5.

true Queen of the Sciences is not philosophy but supernatural theology. In one sense we might say that mathematics is the Queen of the Sciences because it is the most certain of all the sciences. Subjectively, theology is not the most certain of the sciences because it attains knowledge by the light of faith by which, as it were, "we see now through a glass in a dark manner" (1 Cor 13:12). Objectively, however, it is the most certain of the sciences because the source of revealed truth is the divine intellect, which cannot err, whereas the foundation of mathematics and the other sciences is the human mind, which can err.

From the standpoint of its object, theology is also the Queen of the Sciences because its object is God Himself, who transcends human reason, whereas the objects of the other sciences fall within reason's grasp. Therefore, on account of the nobility, sublimity and excellence of its object, the title, "Queen of the Sciences," is rightly ascribed, not to philosophy or mathematics, but to supernatural theology.

Although Saint Thomas does not consider philosophy the noblest or the Queen of the Sciences, he puts a heavy weight on the status of philosophy as *wisdom*. To the extent that philosophy, especially its branch called *metaphysics*, is a knowledge of the highest causes, then it is the "Ruler of the Sciences," *scientiarum rectrix*.[13] Next only to supernatural theology, which is its Queen, metaphysics rules the other sciences. Firstly, because it directs the practice of all the arts toward the perfection and happiness of man. Secondly, because it defends the common axioms and presuppositions of the sciences. Finally, because it regulates the sciences by distinguishing their proper objects and assigning them their respective places in the spectrum of human knowledge.[14]

---

[13] See Saint Thomas Aquinas, *Exposition of Aristotle's Metaphysics*, Prologue, Tr. by Vernon J. Bourke in *The Pocket Aquinas*, p. 145.

[14] Jacques Maritain, *An Introduction to Philosophy* (New York: Sheed & Ward, 1934) Part I, Ch. 6, p. 114. Tr. by E.I. Watkin.

What Is Philosophy?

PHILOSOPHY AND THE EXPERIMENTAL SCIENCES

Philosophy is the science of all things *by their first causes*. This means that philosophy begins by asking "Why?" Or "What explains this being?" After finding the answer to this question, it keeps asking "Why?" until it finds the ultimate answer, or until it has pushed the inquiry as far as the human mind can carry it. If something, say *A*, is contingent on another being *B*, then philosophy asks whether *B* itself is a contingent being. If it finds that *B* is contingent on another being *C*, it again asks why *C* exists. The process continues until it ultimately finds something that requires no other being besides itself to explain it. It is this search for the ultimate reason that merits for philosophy the name "wisdom." Wisdom is not merely certain knowledge, but profound knowledge. It is not merely a science of causes, but a science of the *first* and *highest* causes.

The search for the ultimate reason is the main feature that distinguishes philosophy from physics, biology and the various sciences of phenomena. Although these sciences also deal with contingent beings, they do not carry on their search beyond a knowledge of immediate or secondary causes. Their goal is merely to describe contingent reality in measurable terms or by its observable features. Their object is not contingent being *as being*, but contingent being *as measurable* or *as observable*. On the other hand, the goal of philosophy is not merely to describe, but to *explain* contingent being. It seeks to find the *ultimate* explanation or cause of the actual *existence* of contingent reality.

In astronomy, following the discovery that the universe was expanding, physicists proposed several theories to describe the origin and formation of the universe. According to one school of thought the universe has been expanding from eternity. The continuous creation of new matter maintains it in a steady state by filling the voids left by the expanding galaxies (steady-state theory).[15]

---

[15] For the details of this theory, see Fred Hoyle, *The Nature of the Universe* (New York: Harper & Brothers, 1951).

According to another school of thought the universe has been alternately expanding and contracting (pulsating universe theory). This theory suggests that during the last contraction (approximately 20 billion years ago), the whole universe was "squeezed" into a super-dense, super-hot mass of gas. This mass of "concentrated matter" eventually underwent a big explosion (the Big Bang) that started the great cosmic expansion.[16] There is a popular conjecture among scientists that, considering the present rate of expansion of the universe, the world might not contract anymore but just go on expanding.[17]

All these are very interesting *scientific* theories, but from the standpoint of the philosopher, the knowledge it gives us is not deep enough. The first question that should be asked is not *how* or *when* the universe started to expand or contract, but *why* there was a universe to begin with. In the phraseology of Leibnitz, "Why is there being rather than nothing?" Once this question is raised, the search for ultimate principles begins.

The experimental sciences are mostly descriptive and only partly explanatory. To the extent that they do not discover the first causes of things, they fall far short of explanatory power. They *describe*, rather than explain, physical reality. For example, Newton's equation, $F = G \, m_1 m_2 / s^2$, does not explain why natural bodies attract each other. It only describes how the gravitational force F mathematically relates the masses m_1 and m_2 of the two bodies and the distance s between them. It is a description, not an explanation, of physical reality.

On the other hand, philosophy does not merely seek to describe, but to explain reality. Aristotle's hylemorphic doctrine is not a mere description of *how* bodies change. As a scientific description, it is a bad one. Rather, it is an attempt to explain the

---

[16] The exact age of the universe measured from the last contraction is unknown. Estimates vary according to the method and theory used.

[17] George Gamow, *One, Two, Three... Infinity* (Mentor Books, 1947), p. 313.

essentially mutable character of bodies in terms of their first principles — *matter* and *form*. It is a good philosophical explanation, for it focuses on the core of physical reality and grasps the first principles behind the appearances described by the scientists.

Somebody once stated that the difference between physics and philosophy is that physics is peripheral, while philosophy is central. In one sense this is true. For a physicist seeks to describe a bodily object in terms of observable features that are outside the object's nature, whereas the philosopher's main concern has to do with the object's essence. However, if the statement means that a physicist, *as physicist*, does not seek to know the object's essence, but only to describe its proper accidents, then the statement is definitely wrong. A physicist also seeks to know essences; for example, that of the Oxygen atom. The trouble is that the physicist, or even the philosopher, does not have a direct vision of the essence of the Oxygen atom. So, he has to describe the essence of the Oxygen atom in terms of characteristics that are most distinctive of Oxygen as a substance.

The individual essence of bodily things is a secret of nature that is concealed from both the philosopher and the physicist. To define the Oxygen atom, even the philosopher has to do it in the manner of the physicist, that is, by describing its distinctive, observable characteristics. The real distinction between physics and philosophy is not that physics seeks only the observable characteristics of bodily substance, while philosophy seeks the unobserved essence. Actually, both scientists and philosophers seek the essences of bodily things. They both ask the question, "What is it?" The difference between them is in the profoundness of their questions. In asking the question "What?" the physicist merely seeks a fitting description of the object that serves as a surrogate essence of the object for him. In contrast, the philosopher does not merely ask what Oxygen is, or what Mercury is. What he seeks is not the nature of *this* or *that* body. His questions are more profound than that. He wants to know what is the nature of bodies *as bodies*. What

15

ultimately constitutes the nature of bodily being? Is it its inertia? Its bulk? These are the questions that the philosopher asks.

Since physics and the other sciences of phenomena do not seek to explain being *as being*, but only aim to find a fitting description of measurable or observable being, therefore they cannot answer the ultimate questions that philosophy asks. For example, physics may be able to measure time, or it may be able to give a mathematical description of motion. But it has no answer to such questions as, "What is time?" or "What is motion?" Any scientist who attempts to answer these questions has to do it as a philosopher, not as a scientist.

Also, since the sciences of phenomena do not pursue a knowledge of the highest causes (including final causes), they also have no answers to questions of ultimate significance, such as questions about the meaning and purpose of human life, or of what is morally good or evil, or what makes human actions morally just or unjust. These are philosophical questions that can only be answered by reference to the ultimate purpose of human existence.

Now, if philosophy is a science that seeks, and finds, the answers to questions that physics, chemistry, biology and the other empirical sciences cannot answer, then it is clearly a branch of knowledge that is distinct from the rest of the sciences of phenomena. Therefore, human knowledge does not consist only of the empirical sciences. It also includes philosophy as an equally respectable branch of knowledge that seeks and finds answers to the ultimate questions that the other sciences cannot answer.

The Method of Philosophy

Philosophy is the science of all things by their first causes, *to the extent that it is attainable by the natural light of reason.* The last phrase indicates that philosophy seeks the first causes of things as far as they can be rationally established by the human mind unaided by divine revelation. Even Christian philosophy, which derives inspiration from theological issues, does not prove its conclusions by premises borrowed from divine revelation. The last court of appeal in philosophy, as in any natural science, is objective evidence and logical reasoning, not the authority of the Sacred Scriptures.

Philosophy is a *human science*. Although it treats of God and divine matters, it does so only to the extent that their knowledge is humanly possible to attain. Philosophy does not claim to know truths regarding God and heavenly things that are strictly supernatural, such as the mystery of the Blessed Trinity, the Incarnation and the Redemption. This type of knowledge is altogether beyond its reach and something that no man can justly hope to attain without the aid of divine revelation. Besides strictly supernatural truths, however, there are also truths about God and spiritual things that unaided human reason can reach, such as the truth about God's existence, His attributes, His action upon the world, etc. These matters properly fall within the scope of philosophy.

In saying that philosophy is a science attainable "by reason," we do not mean to exclude from philosophy the role that experience plays in the search for truth. Like mathematics, philosophy is "armchair thinking," but like any human science (including mathematics), philosophy also derives its data from sense-experience. However, there is this difference. Philosophy does not derive its principles from experiences that are accessible only to a few laboratory investigators. Rather, philosophy derives its primary notions from the *common experience* of humankind. The primary sensible data, from which the search for ultimate principles begins, consist of ordinary experiences that are had by everyone, such as the experience of moving or remaining at rest, the experience of growing, of seeing, feeling, thinking and loving. These are common experiences that people in all places have, and on which they build their primary philosophical notions. In contrast, the sciences of phenomena discover their principles, or "laws," by a special process of investigation. The experience arising from this effort is an extraordinary experience available only to the investigator himself. Such, for example, are the experimental observations made by chemists in the laboratory, or the celestial observations made by astronomers through their telescopes, or the amazing observations made by explorers in their expeditions, or even the painstaking research that historians make in their search for historical truth. Because these experiences are not ordinarily available to everyone, we call them *special* experiences.

Unlike the scientist, the philosopher does not have to make a special investigation or perform special experimentation to collect data for philosophical reflection. The facts he needs are already available to him. They consist of his own day-to-day experiences. George Santayana refers to these experiences as "public experiences,"[18] as opposed to the "private experiences" of a scientific investigator. *My* dream is a purely private experience. Nobody else could talk about it but myself. But dreams in general are public experiences. They are experienced by everyone in their sleep. So, we say that dreams belong to the *common experience* of human-kind. Because they are experienced by everyone, the philosopher could talk about them with everyone. On the other hand, my dream is my special experience. It may be a psychoanalyst's object of special investigation, but it could hardly serve as evidence in a philosophical conversation.

Since philosophy does not borrow its principles from physics, but derives them directly from the facts of common experience, philosophy is an *autonomous science*. Philosophy may use scientific facts to illustrate its principles, but its principles and conclusions are intrinsically independent of them. This is why changes in scientific theories do not necessarily invalidate philosophical con-

---

[18] George Santayana, *Skepticism and Animal Faith* (New York: Charles Scribner's Sons, 1923), pp. ix-x.

clusions. The Copernican revolution did not necessarily overthrow Aristotle's philosophy of nature.[19] And the various modes that scientific psychology has taken over the years did not necessarily render Saint Thomas' teachings on the soul obsolete. Not that philosophical theories are immutable, but any change in philosophical theory proceeds, not from the discoveries and findings of science, but from the movements in philosophical inquiry itself.

Philosophy does not differ from the sciences of phenomena only by the fact that its method requires no preliminary gathering or investigation of data. It also differs from the scientific method in the way that it tests its theories and conclusions. Like the sciences of phenomena and unlike mathematics, philosophy verifies its theories in sense experience. But this method of testing a philosophical theory, which Mortimer Adler calls the "empirical test" in philosophy,[20] does not consist in making special experiments. Such a procedure belongs more to the sciences of phenomena, than to philosophy. In philosophy the empirical test simply consists in checking whether the philosophical theory in practice squares with the facts of life and common sense. In other words, philosophy verifies its theories by returning to the same common experience that led to its principles. By evaluating their consequences against the facts of common experience, philosophy can test the strength of such ideologies as idealism, determinism, relativism, etc.

---

[19] However, it did overthrow Aristotle's speculations that were based on ancient physics. We call these science-based theoretical speculations "philosophical myths," rather than philosophy.

[20] See Mortimer J. Adler, *The Conditions of Philosophy* (New York: Atheneum, 1965), Ch. 9.

Chapter Two

Challenges to Philosophy

Many scholars have challenged the definition of philosophy given in the preceding chapter. In this chapter we shall address their criticisms briefly and shall show that the traditional definition of philosophy is indeed appropriate.

THE SCANDAL OF PHILOSOPHY

The first criticism arises from the lack of agreement among philosophers. The conflicting views of those who call themselves "lovers of wisdom" are profoundly disturbing, for they cast doubt on the scientific status of philosophy itself. Scientific knowledge aims at certitude. But certitude on philosophical matters seems impossible. In spite of several centuries of philosophical reflection and debate, philosophers have not reached a consensus regarding the nature of things and the ends of human life. Thus, Aristotle's views did not agree with those of Plato. The ethical teachings of Epicurus did not agree with those of Aristotle. There was no common philosophy even among the great Doctors of the Middle Ages. Saint Bonaventure was no follower of Saint Thomas, and Duns Scotus held a metaphysical doctrine that was different from that of Saint Bonaventure or Saint Thomas. This disparity in thought is also apparent in modern philosophy. The philosophical system of

Spinoza was different from that of Leibnitz. The views of Hume and Berkeley were as opposed to each other as those of Marx and Whitehead. In contrast, physicists and mathematicians frequently agree about their principles, and where there is doubt, they eventually settle their differences within a reasonable amount of time.

In answer to the above criticism, we say that it is not fair to judge the scientific status of philosophy by the difficulty that philosophers have in conforming with each other. Agreement among philosophers is more difficult to obtain because philosophical subjects are more difficult and more complicated to handle than subjects in the physical or the mathematical sciences.

Philosophy is more difficult than physics because it deals with matters that are intelligible but beyond the reach of the senses. For example, philosophers have raised the question whether essence is identical with existence. Although both essence and existence are at the core of reality, neither one is a sensible datum. So, the issue is difficult to resolve. In contrast, the physical sciences have the benefit of settling disputes by direct experimental observation.

By comparison to mathematics, philosophy is also more difficult because it deals with concepts that relate to the whole being of things and not merely to their quantitative aspects. The essences of real beings require more effort to disengage and analyze than their quantitative characteristics. For example, it is easier to show the exact mathematical relationship in the time of occurrence between two events than to define precisely what time is. Also, none of the difficulties of philosophical analysis occurs in mathematics. Mathematical propositions are but universal affirmatives. The nature of quantity and the axiom of equality afford the possibility of immediate conversion and direct substitution. We do not find in philosophical arguments the ease of demonstration ordinarily found in mathematics. This is why complete agreement among philosophers is more difficult and takes a much longer time to obtain.

Also, accepting a philosophical conclusion is more than just making an intellectual assent. Philosophical matters that touch the realm of human conscience (ethics and natural theology), relate to the heart and will of man, and not merely to his intellect. Accepting a conclusion on these matters frequently involves making a commitment. For example, the proposition, "God exists," once accepted, will have a dramatic impact on the thinker's moral life. Similarly, a thinker who acknowledges that the human fetus is a person ought to condemn abortion and defend the rights of the unborn. If a thinker is not ready to accept the resultant obligations and moral consequences of a philosophical conclusion, the chances are that he will reject it. In a world inhabited by people who are *free* to make or not to make a commitment, unanimous agreement is very difficult to obtain. Therefore, if philosophers could not reach a consensus on philosophical matters, it is not because certitude in philosophy is impossible, but because the acceptance of a philo- sophical proposition requires *righteousness* and not merely under- standing. Because of the perversity of the human will, some thinkers are prone to be stubborn and to hold erroneous opinions. This is indeed a lamentable scandal, not for philosophy itself but for fallen man. There are persons of great ability who will deny a proposition that is plainly true, or maintain one that is manifestly false, just to protect their prejudices. Jonathan Swift rightly ob- served, "There is nothing so extravagant or irrational which some philosophers have not maintained for truth."[1]

PHILOSOPHY AND LINGUISTIC ANALYSIS

The second criticism arises from a dispute regarding the object of philosophy. The objection comes from Ludwig Wittgenstein and other linguistic philosophers, who say that philosophy should not

---

[1] Jonathan Swift, *Gulliver's Travels*, Part III, Ch. 6. in Vol. 36 of *Great Books* (Encyclopædia Britannica Inc., 1952), p. 112.

be concerned with things but only with the clarification of thought and language. They say that the natural sciences already deal with the world. So, another science of the world is unnecessary. Besides, disputes often arise because there is a certain opaqueness in our thoughts or some obscurity in the meaning of our words. If we clarify our thoughts and the language that expresses our thoughts, then most so-called "problems" of philosophy will vanish. Therefore, the function of philosophy should be the clarification of thoughts and words, not the investigation of reality. Philosophy should engage in the *pursuit of meaning* rather than the *pursuit of wisdom*.

Although the natural sciences deal with the world of nature, they do not carry on their investigation beyond the knowledge of immediate or secondary causes. Without a knowledge of first causes, the account given by scientists regarding the nature and origin of the world is not wholly satisfying. For, to borrow a metaphor from Kierkegaard, "the knot is not tied at the end of the thread." Therefore, a knowledge of first causes is necessary to complete our understanding of reality. It is necessary for the perfection of knowledge that, besides the natural sciences, there also should be a science of things by their first causes, which is philosophy.

It was Bertrand Russell himself, Wittgenstein's former professor, who reacted strongly against the view that philosophy should concern itself exclusively with the clarification of thought and language. He criticized the linguistic philosophers, particularly Neurath, Hempel, and Carnap, saying, "The new philosophy seems to me to have abandoned, without necessity that grave and important task which philosophy throughout the ages has hitherto pursued. Philosophers from Thales onwards have tried to understand the world . . . I cannot feel that the new philosophy is carrying on this tradition."[2]

---

[2] Bertrand Russell, *My Philosophical Development* (Simon & Schuster, 1959), p. 230.

The English philosopher of science, Sir Karl Popper, also held that the whole linguistic enterprise was misguided. It reduces philosophy to semantics. In a BBC interview with Strawson and Warnock, he said that if we merely polish our language but not talk about the world, then we are metaphorically cleaning our spectacles but not looking through them at the world.

Therefore, the function of philosophy is to understand reality and not merely to clarify thought or language. This is not a reaction against clarity itself. Clarity in thought and expression has always been an ideal that thinkers sought to attain. Even Saint Thomas Aquinas employed some linguistic analysis to clarify the language that Christians used in speaking about God. For example, he analyzed what they meant when they said that God was good and wise.[3] For this purpose, he developed his famous doctrine on analogical predication.

PHILOSOPHY AND EMPIRICISM

The third challenge comes from David Hume and other empiricists who wanted to restrict philosophy to the investigation of sensible reality. They say that philosophy need not deal with *all* contingent beings (which would include non-sensible beings), but only with the material world. For our knowledge starts from sense-experience, and everything that we know is about things that we have experienced. From our sense-experiences we cannot legitimately infer anything concerning the properties, the essence or the existence of anything supra-sensible. Therefore, the investigation of supra-sensible reality in philosophy is unjustifiable.

Although all our knowledge starts from sense-experience, it does not follow that sense-data alone are all that we know. For example, our knowledge of cause-and-effect, so necessary in the

---

[3] See Saint Thomas Aquinas, *Summa Theologica*, Part I, Q. 13.

development of the natural sciences, is something beyond the power of the senses to reach. We have no sense perception of causes *as causes*, or of events as necessarily connected to a cause. Still, when we perceive a lighted candle followed by paper burning, we *know* that the lighted candle is not merely the antecedent, but the cause, of the paper's burning. We know *by our minds* that causality exists and is at work in the world. In seeing one ball strike another, a boy is conscious that the motion of the first ball is a real cause of the second ball's motion. In striking the keys of a piano, the pianist is sure that his movement is a real cause of the music. Whenever we perceive change, as in seeing a ball strike another, we are not merely aware of a simple succession of events, which is all that we would know if our experience were purely sensory. We are also aware of the causal relation. Although we perceive by our senses that A follows B, we simultaneously perceive by our *minds* that A follows B *because* B is the cause of A. To say, as David Hume says, that we merely have a knowledge of antecedents and constant consequents, is to have a distorted notion of human cognition. Human knowledge is at once both sensory and intellectual. In the perception of change we perceive not merely the temporal succession of events, but also their intelligible causal connections.

Therefore, it is not true to say that people have no knowledge of non-sensible reality. Besides causality, there are actually many other supra-sensible realities that we are aware of, such as existence, freedom, friendship, etc.

David Hume insists that our knowledge is purely sensory, and that we have no genuine knowledge of supra-sensible realities, such as cause-and-effect. He says that what we call causality is nothing but the psychological result of our observation that an event invariably follows another. Because we observe that A always follows B, we spontaneously but erroneously think that B is the "cause" of A. There is no causality here, he says, but only an *invariable sequence* of events. Other empiricists say that there is no causality in the world, but only a *necessary succession* of events.

If what we call causality is nothing more than a constant or invariable sequence of events, then we would call any invariable sequence a cause-and-effect relation. This is obviously not so. Although we observe that night invariably follows day, we never say that day is the cause of night. To use Bertrand Russell's metaphor, even if a rooster were to crow every morning before dawn, no one would think that it causes the daybreak to occur. Therefore, although we perceive by our senses many invariable sequences in nature, we do not always perceive in them a causal relation. This is because in any given case it is by our *mind*, and not merely by our senses, that we perceive the presence or absence of a cause-and-effect relation.

Neither could the empiricist hide the absurdity of his position by invoking "necessary succession" as a substitute for causality. We can ask, what about *necessity* itself? Does it belong to the realm of sense? By what sense do we perceive that *A* is a "necessary" consequence of *B*? So, we come back to the fundamental fallacy involved in this foolish denial of man's capacity to perceive non-sensible data. Necessity and contingency are, like causality, supra-sensible conditions that are open only to the perception of the mind. Therefore, man's knowledge of reality extends beyond what can be perceived by the senses. There are also non-sensible data that man by his mind can perceive. If this is the case, then there is no need to restrict the range of philosophy to the realm of the sensible world. One may say, as the ancients did, that the range of philosophy is the *whole* contingent reality.

PHILOSOPHY AND LOGICAL POSITIVISM

The next criticism comes from A.J. Ayer and other logical positivists who base their arguments on the *verifiability criterion of meaning*. According to this criterion a statement is factually significant if, and only if, we know how to verify its truth empirically.

This means that a proposition is meaningful only if some empirical test is available that would allow us under certain conditions to accept the proposition as true, or reject it as false. Moritz Schlick gave an interesting example. Suppose somebody said, "The universe is shrinking uniformly," and by "uniformly" he meant that all things, including our measuring instruments, were shrinking at the same rate. Then nobody could contest the truth of this assertion. For there would be no way of measuring the difference between things before the universe had shrunk and things after it had. Because the statement is unverifiable, it is not factually significant. In contrast, a statement, such as "There are green people on Mars," may be *unverified*, or even false, but inasmuch as it is verifiable "in principle," it is considered meaningful.[4]

Invoking the verifiability principle, the enemies of metaphysics claim that the search for the first causes of things is futile. Since the properties and characteristics of ultimate realities, such as "God" or the "soul," could not be verified by observation, they say that any talk about them amounts to nonsense. Someone suggested that a man who seeks the first causes of things is like "a blind man in a dark room looking for a black hat that is not there."[5]

Logical positivists base their objection on the principle of verification. We now ask, what about *that* principle itself? Is it an empirically verifiable principle? Logical positivists are often embarrassed when we remind them that the principle of verification is itself a proposition that is not empirically verifiable. Therefore, by force of that principle, it also should be regarded as meaningless.

Following Bertrand Russell's *theory of types*, the logical positivists sought a way out of this contradiction by saying that no

---

[4] Professor Karl Popper uses *falsifiability* rather than *verifiability* as the test for a scientific theory. For him, a theory that is not empirically falsifiable is not scientific.

[5] This analogy was quoted by William James in his essay, *Some Problems of Philosophy*.

statement can really say anything about itself. A statement about other statements is a statement of a different class or type from that of the statements spoken of. Therefore, they say, the principle of verification is not itself included among the principles that need to be empirically verifiable. The criterion of verification is not a *logical proposition* that is true or false, but only a *rule* that should be observed.

But why apply such an artificial rule? Why restrict the range of meaningful statements to those that are empirically verifiable? The statement, "God can make a square circle," may be a false statement, but definitely not meaningless. The only statements that are truly meaningless are those that signify nothing, like the statement, "Sensation is more vertical than reason." This statement is meaningless, not because it could not be verified empirically, but because there is nothing to verify. The statement makes no sense. However, philosophical statements, such as "God exists" or "The human soul is immortal," are not of this type because these statements *say* something.[6] The truth of what they say may not be obvious, so they need to be proved. It does not mean that because they could not be proved empirically, then they have no meaning at all. All it means is that laboratory techniques are either not sufficient or are not the appropriate means to establish their truth.

There is nothing wrong when a positivist wishes to limit his investigation of reality to the realm of sense. But if, consequently, he were to declare that any talk about the supra-sensible world is meaningless, then his attitude reveals an intellectual short-sightedness.

Many scientists since Einstein have actually expressed this attitude. Albert Einstein only said that what cannot be measured by

---

[6] Some authors argue that the existence of God may not be unverifiable because the soul after death may have a direct experience of the Deity. See John Hick, "Religious Statements as Factually Significant," *The Existence of God* (Macmillan Publishing Co., 1964), pp. 252-274.

the physicist has no meaning for the physicist *as physicist*. But many scientists have changed that statement to mean that what is not measurable by scientists *does not exist in reality*. This is no less ridiculous than the attitude of a businessman who, after deciding to restrict his interests to economics, declares that any talk that is not related to the world of supply and demand is meaningless. Such statements are absurd. To say that the supra-sensible world does not exist is baseless. Anybody who says that our knowledge must not extend beyond this material world, implies *in fact* that he has crossed the limits of this material world. He has explored the world beyond the realm of sense and, therefore, he could dogmatically deny that there is anything that we could meaningfully discuss about it. This is what Bradley meant when he said that anybody who tries to prove that metaphysics is impossible is a rival metaphysician with a theory of his own.[7]

BERTRAND RUSSELL'S ATTACK

The next objection is an attack against Christian philosophy. Its basis is the mistaken view that to be positively influenced by religious beliefs is inconsistent with the nature of philosophy. For instance, Bertrand Russell criticized Saint Thomas, saying:

> There is little of the true philosophic spirit in Aquinas. He does not, like the Platonic Socrates, set out to follow wherever the argument leads. He is not engaged in an inquiry, the result of which it is impossible to know in advance. Before he begins to philosophize, he already knows the truth; it is declared in the Catholic faith. If he can find apparently rational arguments for some parts of the faith, so much the better; if he cannot, he needs only

---

[7] F.H. Bradley, *Appearance and Reality* (London, 1893; 2nd ed., 9th printing, Oxford: Clarendon Press, 1930).

fall back on revelation. The finding of arguments for a conclusion given in advance is not philosophy but special pleading. I cannot, therefore, feel he deserves to be put on a level with the best philosophers either of Greece or modern times.[8]

This criticism does not have a sound basis. In his *Summa Theologica* Saint Thomas asked "Whether the Universe of Creatures Always Existed?"[9] He raised the question as a reaction to Aristotle who argued in favor of the thesis that the world was everlasting. As a *theologian* Saint Thomas knew from revelation that the world had a beginning in time. But as a *philosopher*, he did not tailor an "apparently rational argument" just to prove what he accepted on faith. He discouraged us from doing such a thing, "lest anyone, presuming to demonstrate what is of faith, should bring forward reasons that are not cogent, so as to give occasion to unbelievers to laugh, thinking that on such grounds we believe things that are of faith."[10] After a more thorough deduction of the same principles used by Aristotle, Saint Thomas showed that reason alone could neither prove nor disprove that the universe always existed.

It is also false to say of Saint Thomas that he merely "fell back on revelation" when he could not find arguments in support of his faith. Although he knew the answer from revelation, Saint Thomas did not use revelation to refute the arguments against it. Instead, he met reason with reason. He refuted Aristotle's original arguments by a more rigorous analysis of what logically follows from his original premises.

Also, Saint Thomas did not have the habit of fabricating arguments to demonstrate revealed truths that are strictly

---

[8] Bertrand Russell, *History of Western Philosophy* (London, G. Allen and Unwin, Ltd., 1946), pp. 484-485.

[9] Saint Thomas Aquinas, *Summa Theologica*, Part I, Question 46, Art. 1.

[10] Saint Thomas Aquinas, *Summa Theologica*, Part I, Question 46, Art. 2.

undemonstrable.[11] In fact, he boldly rejected all arguments that claim to demonstrate the articles of faith, even when these arguments were proposed by holy people.[12] What Saint Thomas said about strictly supernatural truths was that we could only *defend* them, but we could not demonstrate them. At best, he said, we could show that the mysteries of faith were "fitting," "convenient" or "probable."

Bertrand Russell said, "The finding of arguments for a conclusion given in advance is not philosophy but special pleading." But, we ask, is this not also what mathematicians sometimes do? In one of his books Bertrand Russell himself developed a proof for the proposition "$1 + 1 = 2$."[13] Surely, Bertrand Russell knew this fact long before he thought of proving it. Why then does he not regard this a type of "special pleading"? So, what truly matters to a philosopher or a mathematician is not whether he knew the conclusion ahead of the proof, but whether the proof itself stands on solid ground.

Bertrand Russell said that there was little of the true philosophic spirit in Saint Thomas because, unlike Socrates, Saint Thomas would not follow the thread of an argument wherever it leads. On the contrary, we should say that there was so much of the true philosophic spirit in Saint Thomas that he was ready to seek the truth wherever it may be found — yes, even if it is from Sacred Scriptures.

---

[11] In the present terminology a demonstration, as opposed to a mere proof, is an argument so strong that it compels the mind to accept the conclusion as true.

[12] In the *Summa Theologica*, II-II, Q. 1, Art. 5, Reply to Obj. 2, Saint Thomas wrote: "The reasons employed by holy men to prove things that are of faith, are not demonstrations." Tr. by the Fathers of the English Dominican Province (Benziger Brothers, Inc. 1947), Vol. 2, p. 1172.

[13] Bertrand Russell and Alfred North Whitehead, *Principia Mathematica* (3 Vols.; Cambridge University Press, 1910-1913; 2nd ed. 1925-1927), Section 54.43.

Chapter Three

The Goal of Philosophy

Why do people philosophize? Gotthold E. Lessing and other scholars think that people search for the ultimate truth for the sheer joy of searching. For them, the attainment of truth cannot be the goal of philosophy because the possession of truth seems to herald the end of the mind's activity. They maintain that the search for truth, not the possession of it, is the true aim of philosophy.

The above statements betray a distorted view of knowledge. Knowledge is an act. Therefore, to know truth is to act rather than to cease acting. Far from representing the end of the mind's activity, the knowledge or possession of truth manifests the vitality of the intellect or its capacity for immanent action.

Also, in the hierarchy of goods the end is better than the means because we seek the means only *for the sake of the end.* Therefore, it is foolish to think that the unceasing quest of truth is better than the possession of it, just as it is foolish to think that the combat is more important than the victory, for victory is the end or purpose of the battle.

The goal of any science is not the quest, but the possession, of truth. In philosophy the goal is the possession of the highest truth or the *contemplation* of wisdom. To contemplate means not merely to know the truth or to possess it, but also to relish or enjoy it. Philosophy seeks knowledge, not just because knowledge is useful, but primarily because knowledge is delightful. Of everything that pleases the human mind, wisdom — or the knowledge of things by their first causes — gives the greatest joy. Wisdom removes all doubt, puts the mind to rest, and affords a unified vision of reality that is at once harmonious, beautiful and clear. Therefore, philosophy pursues wisdom *for its own sake* as an object of delight and not as a means to a further end.

Francis Bacon and the advocates of dialectical materialism claim that the goal of philosophy is not to contemplate wisdom but to transform the world. They say that philosophy is essentially practical: an instrument for action. Thus, wrote Karl Marx, "Philosophers have only *interpreted* the world in various ways; the point is to *change* it."[1] Also, some scholars deny that any knowledge that does not lead to useful consequences is of any value. They advise philosophers to get down from their Ivory Tower and engage in some useful and practical work rather than just sit in an armchair and dream.

Against these views we maintain that the aim of the philosopher, as philosopher, is to contemplate wisdom — not to work for practical results. Aristotle, whom Dante calls "the Master of those who know,"[2] explains that the nobility of wisdom consists in the fact that it is sought for its own sake and not for the sake of an end beyond itself. If the aim is to produce useful results — that is, results that satisfy our material and temporal needs — then the natural sciences would be enough. A knowledge of secondary causes generally suffices to let us harness the forces of nature. Therefore, if one still seeks, beyond this knowledge, a knowledge of *first* causes, then one is pursuing truth, not just for the satisfaction of some temporal need, but for its own sake.[3]

---

[1] Karl Marx, *Theses on Feuerbach*, last thesis, 1845 — as found in *The Portable Karl Marx* (Penguin Books, 1983), ed. Eugene Kamenka, p. 158.

[2] Dante, *Inferno*, IV, 130. Tr by Charles Eliot Norton in Vol. 21 of *Great Books* (Encyclopædia Britannica, Inc., 1952), p. 6.

[3] Aristotle, *Metaphysics*, 982b 20-25.

The Goal of Philosophy

As a human being, a philosopher may have ends other than contemplation; for example, he may teach to reform society. But as a philosopher, his primary responsibility is toward the contemplation of truth, not toward any other activity. In this sense, the aim of philosophy is similar to that of the Fine Arts. Like truth, beauty can be an object of contemplation. As a human being, an artist may make an artifact to earn his livelihood. But precisely as an artist, his responsibility is to produce a thing of beauty, not to make a living. His work ought to be regulated by the rules of his art, and not, in any manner, by his wage. An artist who, as artist, does not seek beauty for his object, commits a sin against art. Similarly, a philosopher who, as philosopher, does not seek truth for his object, sins against his vocation and corrupts philosophy.

The true philosopher seeks only the contemplation of wisdom. As Saint Thomas Aquinas said, "Truth is a divine thing, a friend more excellent than any human friend."[4] If he compared truth to a friend, it is because we love a friend for his sake, and not for the sake of something else.

Now, how can one say this of Christian philosophy? Is not the aim of Christian philosophy to serve the interest of theology rather than the contemplation of wisdom? Also, if Christian philosophy is philosophy itself in its ministerial role as "handmaid" of theology, then how can we regard it as Ruler of the Sciences?

Paradoxically, to be Ruler of the Sciences and at the same time a handmaid of theology is a valid description of both the nature and the dignity of Christian philosophy. As philosophy, the aim of Christian philosophy is the contemplation of wisdom. In its role as handmaid of theology, philosophy serves, not a lower science or art, but a higher kind of wisdom. Just as the senses are enhanced when they work in the service of a higher power, which is the

---

[4] Saint Thomas Aquinas, *Exposition of Aristotle's Ethics*, I, lect. 6. Tr. by Thomas Gilby in *Saint Thomas Aquinas: Philosophical Texts* (NY: Oxford University Press), p. 36.

intellect, so philosophy is ennobled rather than disgraced when it plays its role as handmaid of theology. No other science deserves to render this service. To be chosen for this office is the highest honor worthy only of a ruler, for the ruler is the first of the Queen's subjects. Therefore, far from degrading philosophy, to act as handmaid of theology speaks, not of the inferiority, but of the pre-eminence of Christian philosophy over all the other human sciences.

THE VALUE OF PHILOSOPHY

Because philosophy does not aim to produce anything useful or practical, but only to contemplate wisdom, it is clear that, at least in this sense, philosophy is useless. But to speak of philosophy as "useless" in this sense is not to belittle it, but to praise it. The fact that wisdom is sought, not for production or other extrinsic ends but for its own sake, is its dignity.

Philosophy is not useful knowledge. It is rather "free" knowledge. Aristotle explains that "just as a free man is one who exists for his own sake and not for anyone else's, so we study this science as the only one that is free, since it is the only one that is studied for its own sake. For this reason, one would be justified in regarding the possession of it as more than human . . ."[5] This is why philosophy, although not an art, is in the curriculum of the liberal arts, for it serves no other end beyond itself, and is pursued solely for its own sake. In contrast the servile arts are not free. They serve some extrinsic purpose, such as that of satisfying our temporal needs. Thus, engineers study to build bridges or to advance technology. Economists do research to increase production, and doctors to cure

---

[5] Aristotle, *Metaphysics*, 982b 25. Tr. by J.L. Creed in Renford Bambrough's *The Philosophy of Aristotle* (New York: Mentor Books, 1963), p. 44.

diseases. But philosophers study for the love of learning, which culminates in wisdom.

To say that philosophy is not useful (in production or in the satisfaction of our temporal needs) does not mean to say that philosophy lacks value. On the contrary, it is because it is so precious that, like a jewel, it is not to be used, but only to be treasured. Its value is of a different order, higher and above the value of the other intellectual disciplines. In affording a knowledge of the first and highest causes, it is, in a way, divine. That is why Aristotle said that to possess it was "more than human," for its aims go beyond the mere satisfaction of temporal, human needs.

The effort to surpass the limitations of human life has its roots in the very nature of man. That which makes man specifically human is his intellect, which in him is something divine.[6] By his intellect man shares the nature of pure spirits. Spirits have no material cares; wisdom alone is their food. This is also the case with the mind of man. Thus, Saint Thomas says that to live a life of pleasure is beastly; to live the active social life is human; but to live the contemplative life is angelic or "superhuman."[7] Although he or she remains truly human, the contemplative person lives a life better than the purely human life.[8]

Also, to say that philosophy is useless does not mean to say that it does not benefit humankind. It only means that philosophy does not serve ends other than the contemplation of wisdom. But the contemplation of truth is greatly beneficial to man, for it answers the need of man's rational nature. To the extent that it gives man a profound view of reality, and enables him to give a stable orientation to his entire conscious life, it makes him more truly

---

[6] Aristotle, *Nicomachean Ethics*, Book 10, Ch. 7, 1177b 26-28.

[7] Saint Thomas Aquinas, *On the Cardinal Virtues*, Q. 1, Art. 1: *non proprie humana, sed superhumana.*

[8] This is one of Jacques Maritain's favorite expressions: *Vita quae est secundum speculationem est melior quam quae secundum hominem.*

human, indeed "more than human." This is why the pragmatist, who advises us to be concerned exclusively with what would bring useful and practical results, is in a sense being very impractical. Since he values only those things that bring material success, he fails to see the things that most truly serve the interests of man. As Chesterton saw it, the most impractical man is the practical man.

Therefore, philosophy is not altogether useless. It is useless only to those who would not make use of it. Philosophy is useful, but its utility is of a different kind. It is the utility of those things that do not deal with means, but with ends. Philosophy does not provide us with such and such means that would make life more comfortable, but it helps us to understand the *purpose* of life and the very *reasons* for caring, suffering, and hoping.

Science and technology are useful in the sense that they supply us with the *means* to master the forces of nature. In the words of Francis Bacon, "knowledge gives us *power.*" Now, power can be used for good or for evil. Although philosophy does not provide us with power, it teaches us what application of power is good and what is evil. Philosophy helps us decide what use of power serves the ultimate end of human life and what goes against it. Since we measure the goodness of the means in relation to its fitness to serve the end, it is not science but philosophy that tells us what use of power is good and what is evil. It is philosophy that provides direction for action because it alone deals with questions that pertain to the ultimate end or purpose of human existence. Physics does not deal with the ultimate end of human life and, therefore, it cannot answer questions about moral right and wrong. "Good" and "evil" are outside its vocabulary. Here then lies the practical value of philosophy. As Mortimer J. Adler noted, "The more science we possess, the more we need philosophy; for the more power we have, the more we need direction."[9]

---

[9] Mortimer J. Adler, *Great Ideas from the Great Books*, Part I, Ch. 4.

The Goal of Philosophy

THE PHILOSOPHER IN SOCIETY

In *The Republic* Plato said that the person who is most fit to govern the city is the philosopher. If Plato held this view, it is because he thought that the eternal and immutable principles that rule the world were beyond appearances and were attainable only by philosophers. Therefore, as reason must rule the perfect soul, so the philosopher must rule the ideal city. What society needed, he argued, was not democracy, but an aristocratic state ruled by philosophers. *"Until philosophers are kings, or the kings and princes of this world have the spirit and power of philosophy, and political greatness and wisdom meet in one... cities will never have rest from their evils — no, nor the human race."*[10]

Today there are many people who, like Plato, invite philosophers to devote their time to the study and discussion of contemporary social problems. This invitation is valid, for it is fitting for a wise man to give counsel in matters requiring direction. The wise man does not have to rule, but it pertains to his office to teach even the king. Yet, philosophers who wish to discuss practical problems should first acquaint themselves with the nature of their data. Often, the finding of solutions to particular problems requires specialized training and experience not accessible to a philosopher as philosopher. Nothing is more dangerous than a philosopher who thinks himself qualified to solve political problems just because he knows the first causes of things. Even Saint Thomas Aquinas seemed uneasy in advising the rulers of his time. In his letter to the Duchess of Brabant, Saint Thomas wrote: "It would have pleased me had you sought on these points the advice of others more experienced in such matters."[11]

---

[10] Plato, *The Republic*, Book V. Tr. by Benjamin Jowett in Vol. 7 of *Great Books* (Encyclopædia Britannica, Inc., 1952), p. 369.

[11] Tr. by Vernon J. Bourke in *The Pocket Aquinas* (New York: Washington Square Press, 1969), pp. 248-249.

That philosophers become rulers, although possible, is not desirable since it imposes an unnecessary burden and danger to their vocation. As Immanuel Kant said, "That kings should become philosophers, or philosophers kings, can scarce be expected; nor is it to be wished, since the enjoyment of power inevitably corrupts the judgment of reason, and perverts its liberty."[12] To ask a philosopher to assume the responsibilities and power of the king is to punish him. The function of the philosopher *as* philosopher is *to contemplate*, not to rule. His job in society is *to teach* the necessary principles of the social order, not to offer practical solutions to the transitory problems of the city. We agree with Plato that it is desirable for kings and, for that matter, for any man to know philosophy. Yet, we maintain that it is not necessarily true that a philosopher, just because he is a philosopher, is fit to be a king. In the matter of kingship or the government of a city, what we need is not just the virtue of wisdom, but the virtue of *prudence*. This explains the saying attributed to Saint Thomas: "Let the wise teach us, the prudent govern us, and the good pray for us."

---

[12] Immanuel Kant, *Perpetual Peace*, Supplement II. This quotation is from Mortimer Adler and Charles Van Doren, *Great Treasury of Western Thought* (New York: R.R. Bowker Co., 1977), p. 1100.

Chapter Four

The Marks of an Authentic Philosophy

To show the difference between philosophy and its counterfeits, we have to explain the characteristics or marks of an authentic philosophy. There are five marks. First, true philosophy begins in *wonder*, not in doubt. Second, philosophy is dialectical, not mathematical. Third, a genuine philosophy is clear, not esoteric. Fourth, authentic philosophy is perennial, not just contemporary or modern. Fifth, philosophy is open, not closed, to the influence of divine revelation.

PHILOSOPHY BEGINS IN WONDER

When a man is confronted with a mystery, or with something whose causes are still unknown, he wonders why. Such, for Socrates, was the beginning of wisdom. In the *Theaetetus* Plato quotes Socrates as saying, "Wonder is the feeling of a philosopher, and philosophy begins in wonder."[1] Aristotle agrees, saying: "It is owing to their

---

[1] Plato, *Theaetetus*, 155B. Tr. by Benjamin Jowett in Vol. 7 of *Great Books*, p. 519.

wonder that men both now begin and at the first began to philosophize."[2]

In the twentieth century William James repeated this insight, saying that wonder "is the mother of metaphysics."[3] Wonder is really more than this. It is the beginning of all science. Albert Einstein testifies:

> The fairest thing we can experience is the mysterious. It is the fundamental emotion which stands at the cradle of true art and true science. He who knows it not and can no longer wonder, no longer feels amazement, is as good as dead, a snuffed out candle.[4]

What does it mean to wonder? To wonder means to realize that there is something strange behind the things that we ordinarily perceive. To wonder is to notice something extraordinary in the ordinary things we see. For example, there is perhaps nothing more familiar to us than the fact that things exist, but it takes a philosopher like Leibnitz to wonder *why* they do. He was so filled with the wonder of *being* that he momentarily forgot his immediate needs and asked, "Why indeed is there being rather than nothing?" The "eye of the philosopher" made him notice what was most unusual

---

[2] Aristotle, *Metaphysics*, I, 2. 982b 12. Tr. by Richard McKeon in *The Basic Works of Aristotle*, p. 693. Commenting on Aristotle, Saint Thomas also said: "The reason the philosopher is compared to the poet is that both are concerned with wonders." Tr. by John P. Rowan, *Commentary on Aristotle's Metaphysics* (Chicago: Henry Regnery, 1961), Lesson 3.

[3] William James, *Some Problems of Philosophy* (New York: Longmans, Green & Co., 1911), p. 38.

[4] Albert Einstein, *The World As I See It* (New York, Philosophical Library, 1949), p. 5. A collaborator of Einstein also said of him: "From the time Einstein was fifteen or sixteen years old (so he has often told me) he puzzled over the question: what will happen if a man tries to catch a light ray? For years he thought about this very problem. Its solution led to relativity theory. We see in this one example some important features of Einstein's genius. First and above all, there is the capacity for wonder." Leopold Infeld, *Albert Einstein: His Work and Its Influence on Our World* (New York: Scribner's, 1950), p. 41.

in the ordinary things we see: the very being of things *that need not be*.

René Descartes, the Father of Modern Philosophy, thought that *doubt*, not wonder, was the beginning of wisdom. According to him, one must doubt all facts and opinions (except only the fact of one's existence) to rebuild philosophy on a new foundation. What a poor substitute this is for wonder! It is true that wonder, like doubt, implies the absence of perfect knowledge and certitude. However, it does not, like doubt, leave us with no desire to seek further. On the contrary, it is wonder that impels us to go on searching. As Saint Thomas explains, "If a man, knowing the eclipse of the sun, consider that it must be due to some cause, and know not what that cause is, he wonders about it, and *from wondering proceeds to inquire*."[5] Therefore, wonder, more truly than doubt, is the origin of wisdom.

As Joseph Pieper remarked, wonder is not the starting point of philosophy in the simple sense of *initium*, a mere beginning. It is rather a *principium*, a source, the wellspring of philosophy.[6] Wonder does not merely initiate the search for knowledge, but motivates the philosopher to keep on searching and ask more questions. There is no end to this search because truth, like being, is inexhaustible. There is always something more to know. "No philosopher," says Saint Thomas, "has ever been able to discover perfectly the nature of a single fly."[7] In this sense we can say that philosophy will never die, not because we will never find the answers, as the skeptics supposed, but because there are always more things to wonder at, and more sublime things to know.

---

[5] Saint Thomas Aquinas, *Summa Theologica*, Part I-II, Q. 3, Art. 8, at the body of the article. Tr. by the Fathers of the English American Province, *Summa Theologica* (Benziger Brothers, Inc., 1947), Vol. I, p. 602 (Italics added for emphasis).

[6] Joseph Pieper, *Leisure — The Basis of Culture* (Pantheon Books, 1948), Ch. 3. Tr. by Alexander Dru.

[7] Saint Thomas Aquinas, *The Apostle's Creed*. Tr. by Laurence Shapcote in *The Three Greatest Prayers* (Manchester, NH: Sophia Institute Press, 1990), p. 6.

The inexhaustibility of truth is felt not only by philosophers but by scientists and mathematicians as well. For instance, consider the following testimony of one of the greatest men in the history of science, Sir Isaac Newton:

> I do not know what I may appear to the world, but to myself I seem to have been only like a boy playing on the seashore, and diverting myself in now and then finding a smoother pebble or a prettier shell than ordinary, whilst the great ocean of truth lay all undiscovered before me.[8]

Philosophy is Dialectical

Although postulates and theories have a role to play in its development, philosophy *ideally* aims to derive its conclusions from certain principles. This is why in the beginning of this book we said that philosophy is a science as respectable as the sciences of phenomena, for philosophy aims at certitude. However, the certitude that philosophy attains is *not* mathematical certitude, but only the kind of certitude proper to its mode of inquiry, which is often physical or moral certitude.

In the seventeenth century Descartes and Spinoza dreamed to build a philosophical edifice after the manner of mathematics. Not satisfied in discovering a fact with anything less than mathematical certitude, they vainly thought of proving every philosophical proposition *in more geometrico*. For example, Spinoza's *Ethics* has propositions, proofs, corollaries, lemmas, scholiums and the like. The failure of Descartes and Spinoza only shows how inappropriate the mathematical method is in handling the subject matter of philosophy.

In mathematics demonstrations are made by means of the

---

[8] Isaac Newton, *Remarks*, 1727.

formal cause, by deducing consequences that proceed from the definition of mathematical concepts or entities. But in philosophy a demonstration by means of the formal cause is hardly adequate. For the main problem of philosophy is the problem of *existence*. Now, the existence of any being cannot be deduced simply from its definition. It could only be explained by reference to its extrinsic causes, which are the *efficient* and *final cause*. Therefore, the mathematical procedure of demonstrating from the formal cause is inadequate for the purpose that the philosopher has in mind. The dialectical process of tracing the efficient or final cause of a thing is the procedure that is most proper to philosophy, especially the philosophy of nature and moral philosophy. Often, such demonstrations made by means of extrinsic causes do not result in metaphysical, but only in *physical* or *moral* certitude.[9]

Both Aristotle and Saint Thomas warned us not to seek greater certitude in any scientific discipline than the subject matter would allow.[10] The error in the attempt to reduce philosophy to mathematics lies in the fact that it tries to obtain mathematical certitude even on matters where only physical or moral certitude is possible. Of course, the original inspiration of Descartes and Spinoza was not vain. It was nothing other than the desire to present philosophy in an ordered fashion, from the simple to the complex, from the clear to the obscure. Such a goal is always worthy to pursue no matter what style one finally adopts in making a philosophical exposition. However, one must also respect the nature of philosophical inquiry. Although it strives to prove conclusions that are perennially valid, philosophical inquiry is by nature dialectical. Like the other sciences of phenomena, philosophy starts from sense-data. The process of tracing the first principles of

---

[9] See Saint Thomas Aquinas, *Exposition of Boethius on the Trinity*, VI, 1, c. An English translation may be found in Vernon J. Bourke, *The Pocket Aquinas* (New York: Washington Square Press, 1969), pp. 39-40.

[10] See Aristotle, *Nicomachean Ethics*, Bk. I, Ch. 7, 1098a, 25.

nature from the common experience of humankind, is a dialectical process that involves *making assumptions* and *testing them*. It is an error to think that it is possible to rebuild philosophy, like the geometry of Euclid, by starting from a few self-evident principles, and then deduce all philosophical conclusions from them.

Because of this fundamental difference between the mode of philosophical inquiry and the mathematical approach, there also arises this important difference between mathematical conclusions and philosophical conclusions. Mathematical conclusions are inter-connected linearly, which means that one conclusion explains, and helps us understand, the next one. Often, a theorem or conclusion proved in one argument becomes a premise in the next argument. In philosophy conclusions are not interconnected linearly but circularly. Due to the interaction of causes, the conclusion in one argument sometimes adds depth to our understanding of previous conclusions and premises, but without implying a vicious circle.[11]

The success of the quantitative approach in the study of nature led some thinkers to believe that the mathematical approach is the only way to reach certitude. Let us review some incidents to see how this prejudice came about.

Before William Harvey's discovery of the circulation of the blood (1628), people believed the old theory that the blood was the carrier of vital forces in a living animal. According to Galen, a distinguished physician of Antiquity, the stomach first digests the food, which is then carried to the liver. The liver changes the food into blood, which then flows to the heart and into the lungs, where it receives the "breath of life." Finally, the heart pumps the blood into the body where it is used. No circulation of the blood was here recognized. Galen thought that the liver continually created new blood, and the body eventually consumed it.

Harvey tested Galen's hypothesis with a simple experiment.

---

[11] See Saint Thomas Aquinas, *Exposition of Boethius on the Trinity*, V, 1, Reply to Obj. 9. Tr. by Vernon J. Bourke in *The Pocket Aquinas*, p. 152.

Mathematically, the flow of blood in a human body could be calculated by measuring the pulse-rate and the capacity of the heart. So, Harvey asked, "How much blood must the liver produce to account for the observed flow of blood?" By his estimate, the liver would need to generate ten pounds of blood per minute. This means that to produce the observed flow of blood, the liver must produce much more blood than food could supply. This conclusion was clearly absurd. So, Harvey denied Galen's hypothesis, and proposed the possibility that blood circulates throughout the whole body.

The final proof for the circulation of the blood came only with Anton van Leeuwenhoek's invention of the microscope. In 1660 Marcello Malpighi observed through the microscope the capillaries that connected the arteries and the veins, and confirmed Harvey's earlier work. Although this empirical proof came years after Harvey made his conclusion, Harvey's approach dramatically illustrated the power of the quantitative method to test a belief that prevailed in biological thought for more than a thousand years.

Another example that illustrates the power of the quantitative method is Antoine Lavoisier's solution to the problem of combustion. Like Aristotle, George Ernest Stahl wondered about what makes objects burn. He suggested that materials burn because of the liberation of *phlogiston*, a hypothetical "principle of fire." Like Harvey, Lavoisier tested Stahl's hypothesis by asking, "If phlogiston is liberated during combustion, how much weight is lost in the burned substance?" By a series of experiments and careful measurements, Lavoisier discovered that, while burning, the weight of substances such as sulphur and phosphorus actually *increased* rather than decreased (because oxygen was absorbed). This discovery was a fatal blow to the phlogiston theory. It also proved the usefulness of the quantitative approach in science. The new discovery brought new insights not only in chemistry but also in biology, for now we may think of the oxidation in breathing as a chemical process identical to combustion.

From then on scientists regarded quantity as more important than quality for the attainment of certainty in knowledge. Earlier Johann Kepler accepted this view. Sir Isaac Newton also developed his system of classical mechanics in the same spirit. Many thinkers became firm in their opinion that no statement could be certain unless it is formulated in quantitative terms. So, they thought that philosophy also had to be quantitative to be certain.

It seems that no one has stated the ideal of an exclusively mathematical and empirical approach to reality more openly and more forcefully than David Hume. Toward the end of his *Enquiry Concerning Human Understanding*, he wrote:

> When we run over libraries, persuaded of these principles, what havoc must we make? If we take in our hand any volume of divinity or school metaphysics, for instance; let us ask, *Does it contain abstract reasoning concerning quantity and number?* No. *Does it contain any experimental reasoning concerning matter of fact and existence?* No. Commit it then to the flames: for it can contain nothing but sophistry and illusion.[12]

The above remark is an unfortunate one. There is no justification why philosophy cannot be certain simply because its propositions are not expressed in mathematical terms. Even the experimental sciences must be based on a knowledge that is *non-quantitative*. The first conception of a physical theory is always non-mathematical. Einstein tells us so:

> Fundamental ideas play the most essential role in forming physical theory. Books on physics are full of complicated mathematical formulae. But thoughts and ideas, not formulae, are the beginning of every physical theory. The ideas must later take the mathematical form of a quanti-

---

[12] David Hume, *An Enquiry Concerning Human Understanding*, XII, 132. In Vol. 35 of *Great Books*, p. 509.

tative theory, to make possible the comparison with experiment.[13]

Also, measurement always presupposes a certain knowledge of the thing to be measured. If we wish to measure the speed of a car from readings on a speedometer, we must first know *what* speed is and *what* a speedometer is. Unless we first know these, we cannot interpret the readings on the dial correctly. The readings by themselves do not tell us what they point to in reality. They can indicate oil consumption, gas, or electric current as well. Therefore, experiment and measurement presuppose a knowledge of the nature of the thing to be measured. This initial knowledge is *non-quantitative*. Also, it must be *certain*; otherwise, all measurement and all science would be based on uncertain principles.

Therefore, we do not measure first to attain knowledge and certitude. On the contrary, we must have a certain knowledge of nature first before we measure. Often, we only measure to strengthen our understanding, or add detail to our fundamental knowledge, of nature. For example, common experience suffices to tell us that objects fall. But we need to perform experiments and actual measurements to know how fast objects fall or whether they fall in a uniform motion or in an accelerated motion. Unless supplemented by a non-quantitative knowledge, the mathematical approach is in many practical cases also inadequate. To illustrate this, consider the following problem. Suppose that a boy can do a piece of work in 2 days, while another boy can do the same piece of work in 6 days. In how many days could the two boys finish the work together? Viewed simply as a problem in algebra, the answer is 11/ 2 days.[14] In reality, however, the two boys might stop for a while

---

[13] Albert Einstein and Leopold Infeld, *The Evolution of Physics*, (New York: Simon and Schuster, 1938) Part IV, p.277.

[14] Let x = the number of days it will take the boys to do the work together. Then $x/2 + x/6 = 1$, from which $x = 1 1/2$.

to play, or they might chat while they work, so that it probably would take more than 1 1/2 days to do the work. The mathematical estimate, calculated purely by algebra, was wrong precisely because of a neglect to consider the psychology of children. Therefore, in solving human problems mathematics is not enough. One also needs philosophy and other non-quantitative human sciences.

It is a sad and tragic fact that many scientists fell victims to the idolatry of figures. It is to this type of people that Antoine de Saint-Exupéry was referring when he chided the "grown-ups." He said,

> Grown-ups love figures. When you tell them that you have made a new friend, they never ask you any questions about essential matters. They never say to you, "What does his voice sound like? What games does he love best? Does he collect butterflies?" Instead, they demand: "How old is he? How many brothers has he? How much does he weigh? How much money does his father make?" Only from these figures do they think they have learned anything about him. If you were to say to the grown-ups, "I saw a beautiful house made of rosy brick, with geraniums in the windows and doves on the roof," they would not be able to get any idea of that house at all. You would have to say to them, "I saw a house that cost $20,000." Then they would exclaim: "Oh, what a pretty house that is!"[15]

Scientists, who claim that no human investigation is scientific unless it employs mathematics, are like the "grown-ups." They are not interested in anything but numbers.

---

[15] Antoine de Saint-Exupéry, *The Little Prince* (New York: Harcourt Brace Jovanovich, 1943, 1971), pp. 16-17.

The Marks of an Authentic Philosophy

PHILOSOPHY IS CLEAR

This means that philosophy is not *esoteric*. It does not have doctrines that are contrary to the opinions and beliefs of ordinary people. An authentic philosophy does not confuse the mind but enlightens it. It satisfies the *empirical test* and is consistent with the facts of life and logic. For example, a philosophy that maintains against common experience and against the most obvious testimony of common sense that the world is unreal, cannot be a true philosophy. Since it contradicts common experience, it has no place in the universe of human thought.

In the present context "common sense" does not mean hasty judgments based on inadequate observation, or preconceptions adopted unquestioningly from childhood. On the contrary, "common sense" refers to those primary intuitions common to all, which the human mind grasps at the first awakening of thought. By these intuitions we become aware of the existence of the world, of the self, the truth of the principle of non-contradiction, etc. By common sense we apprehend self-evident truths. Therefore, common sense is the root of those genuine certainties and axioms on which true philosophy stands. Common sense is nothing but *human reason* itself in its pre-scientific stage. This is why philosophy should not contradict common sense, although it must always attempt to go beyond it.

Unfortunately, the philosophy that many thinkers propose today contains many strange doctrines that contradict common sense. Some scholars regard this character of contemporary thought, not as a failure, but as the "triumph" of reason over the naiveté of common sense. They fail to see that unintelligibility is not necessarily depth.

51

Philosophy is Perennial

It is perennial because the questions it deals with, and the evidences it uses, are the same for all people always and everywhere. The questions and principles of philosophy arise from the common experience of humankind. So, they do not vary with each passing phase of history, but remain the same from one generation to the next.

No matter how far apart in time and place, philosophers have a certain contemporaneity that scientists at different times and places do not have. Scientific theories are often based on the latest discoveries obtained by the latest equipment. So, scientists of a later generation are truly ahead in terms of basic knowledge than scientists of an earlier generation. Einstein was truly more advanced in basic scientific knowledge than Galileo, and Galileo more advanced than Archimedes. This is not true of philosophers. Philosophers derive their fundamental knowledge of nature from the common experience of humankind. Therefore, as Mortimer Adler used to say, philosophers as far apart in time as Aristotle and William James could deal with the same questions and argue by the same principles. In this sense Mr. Adler rightly said that even the Greeks of the fifth century B.C. were our "contemporaries."

Therefore, the true philosopher reads ancient writings with a sense of the presence of the past. When he writes, he writes not only for the present but also for future generations. The true philosopher sees the whole philosophical tradition of humankind with a sense of continuity. It is this sense of the simultaneous presence of the past and the future in the present moment, this sense of what is timeless in the temporal, that makes the philosopher, and his philosophy, *perennial*.

Because philosophy is perennial, it is also always *relevant*. When someone asked Harry Truman why he was reading Plutarch's *Lives*, he answered, "In order to understand what is going on in Washington." The message is clear. Although ancient, the principles of political philosophy still apply. The fact that many people don't engage in philosophy nowadays obscures the relevance of philosophy in contemporary life. However, what is relevant in our time is not necessarily what the people *want* to do, but what the people *need*. Contemporary man needs, besides material success, the right principles to live by. He needs a philosophy that teaches him how to think right and how to live well. Obviously this philosophy is very relevant.

Since philosophy is perennial, therefore it is traditional. However, this does not mean that philosophy is static. As a developing science, philosophy continues to change. However, changes in philosophy are possible only with regard to its *theories*, not with regard to those axioms and fundamental notions that proceed from our primary intuition of being. Unlike theorems that are certain (since they proceed from self-evident principles), philosophical theories are only *probable* explanations based on plausible principles (postulates). Therefore, changes in philosophy are possible with respect to these theories. Like scientists, philosophers *may* change and update their theories as their understanding of the subject improves with time.

However, the axioms and fundamental notions of philosophy, as well as the conclusions that necessarily proceed from them, have a different status. Considered *objectively*, these principles and the knowledge they convey, are certain and *immutable*. But when regarded *subjectively*, that is, as a knowledge that a person acquires during his lifetime, then even these principles may be regarded as being *in process*. Since the first principles of philosophy do not consist only of easily understood axioms but also of principles from experience, philosophers continually reflect upon these principles to deepen their understanding of them with time. Unlike progress in the experimental sciences, however, where progress often proceeds by the overthrow of one set of principles by another, progress in philosophy proceeds by *deepening insight*.

This deepening results from a greater understanding of the same principles derived from common experience.

Therefore, philosophy is existentially dynamic. Philosophy is alive. It grows by absorbing within itself the insights gained in the thinking of every age. Not ancient or new, but current and living, philosophy has a history as long as that of human reason itself. Philosophy is a continuing dialogue, a "conversation of minds," so to speak, that has been going on from the dawn of reason to the present day.

Even in the arts, where novelty is the rule, a certain tradition is necessary to insure vitality. Mozart testifies:

> People make a mistake who think that my art has come so easily to me. Nobody has devoted so much time and thought to composition as I. There is not a famous master whose music I have not studied over and over.[16]

In the sciences, as in the arts, a continuous tradition is necessary to insure progress. For this reason, truly great scientists give credit to the works of early researchers. Speaking of his new theory of relativity, for example, Einstein paid tribute to Sir Isaac Newton:

> No one must think that Newton's great creation can be overthrown by this or by any other theory. His clear and wide ideas will forever retain their significance as the foundation on which our modern conceptions of physics have been built.[17]

Fulton Sheen said that, as nothing can be more tragic to a man than the loss of his memory, so nothing can be more tragic to a

---

[16] Mozart, as quoted by Joseph Machlis, *The Enjoyment of Music* (New York: Norton, 1963), p. 308.

[17] Albert Einstein, "Time, Space, and Gravitation," *Out of My Later Years* (New York: Philosophical Library, 1950), p. 58.

civilization than the loss of its tradition. Tradition is the underpinning of a flourishing civilization. However, tradition does not merely consist in copying what has gone before. It does not preserve the past for the sake of repetition, but to assert its timelessness. As Igor Stravinsky said,

> A real tradition is not the relic of a past that is irretrievably gone. Far from implying the repetition of what has been, tradition presupposes the reality of what endures.[18]

For the scientist, the artist, and more so for the philosopher, any kind of development requires tradition. In particular, a deepening philosophical understanding of basic principles requires the cooperation of several minds laboring through centuries of reflection and insight. For this reason, a good philosopher respects the thoughts of those who came before him. He listens to their opinions and recognizes their accomplishments. Instead of disregarding the achievements of past masters, he gives them credit for whatever is true in their writings. Bernard of Chartres displays the attitude proper to a good philosopher:

> We are like dwarfs seated on the shoulders of giants. We see more things than the ancients and things more distant, but this is due neither to the sharpness of our sight, nor to the greatness of our stature, it is simply because they have lent us their own.[19]

Unfortunately, modern and contemporary philosophers prefer to build their philosophical systems independently of the past. They make no effort to study profoundly the thoughts of ancient thinkers. They feel that the works of earlier thinkers now have

---

[18] Igor Stravinsky, as quoted by Christoph Gluck, *Composers on Music*, ed. Sam Morgenstern (New York: Bonanza Books, 1956), p.452.

[19] Bernard of Chartres, quoted by John of Salisbury, *Metalogicon*, III, 4 (Translation by Etienne Gilson).

nothing more than historical significance. For example, Francis Bacon said, "It is idle to expect any great advancement in science from the . . . engrafting of new things upon old. We must begin anew from the very foundations."[20] Descartes' new system of philosophy originated with the same spirit. While acknowledging that the study of the ancients may be useful for historical purposes, he warned us, "There is great danger lest in too-absorbed study of those works we should become infected with their errors."[21] He did not trust anybody's opinion. So, he decided to rebuild philosophy on a new foundation. These philosophers forget that in interpreting the data of *common* experience, the earlier philosophers are in a sense our contemporaries. They forget that even in the field of science, modern scientists are not necessarily better in interpreting facts than the ancients; they merely have better facts to interpret.[22]

Due to their obsession for novelty, those who disregard the thoughts of past thinkers are bound to "reinvent the wheel." They also risk repeating old mistakes. This has been the tragedy of philosophy since Descartes. Disregarding the philosophical tradition started by the ancients, modern philosophers unnecessarily go through the same difficulties that our intellectual pioneers encountered. The aberrations in modern and contemporary thought remind us of similar errors committed in the past. For example, the mistakes of Bergson match those of Heraclitus. The errors of Whitehead parallel those of Plato. In having abandoned the efforts of those who have contributed to our philosophical heritage, many modern and contemporary thinkers propose opinions that had long been refuted. Jacques Maritain wisely observed, "A philosophy that is not ancient is very soon old."[23]

---

[20] Francis Bacon, *The New Organon* (Indianapolis: Bobbs-Merrill, 1960), p. 46.

[21] René Descartes, *Philosophical Writings*, ed. Norman K. Smith (New York: Modern Library, 1958) p. 8.

[22] See the explanations by Fulton Sheen, *Old Errors and New Labels* (New York: Kennikat Press, 1970), pp. 157-158.

[23] Jacques Maritain, *Theonas* (New York: Sheed & Ward, 1933), p. 58. Tr. by F.J. Sheed.

The Marks of an Authentic Philosophy

Philosophy is open to the influence of all truth, including scientific and religious truths. Saint Ambrose said that all truth, by whomsoever it is uttered, is from the Holy Spirit: *Omne verum a quocumque dicatur, a Spiritu Sancto est.* Therefore, true philosophy must take advantage of the advances in modern science, even if it itself does not engage in an experimental search for truth. Equally, a genuine philosophy must welcome the aid of divine revelation. A philosophy that works under the influence of theology is a Christian philosophy. In its character as *Christian*, philosophy is not merely compatible with the Christian faith. It also *professedly* and *deliberately seeks* the guidance of divine revelation in the effort to attain truth rationally.

One may see the advantages of a Christian philosophy over a purely natural philosophy by comparing the philosophy of Saint Thomas with that of Aristotle. The difference between them beautifully illustrates the difference between aided and unaided wisdom. Undeniably, Saint Thomas got many of his philosophical views from Aristotle. Saint Thomas himself was not ashamed of the fact. In his theological writings he quoted Aristotle so extensively that he even gave occasion for his critics to say that he was but a "copycat" of Aristotle. But was he really?

Let us compare their views on *metaphysics*. For Aristotle, as for Saint Thomas, there are four causes — the material cause, the formal cause, the efficient cause and the final cause. But for Aristotle, the efficient and final causes of a thing are not necessarily extrinsic to it, for they are sometimes identical to the formal cause, which is intrinsic to the thing.[24] For example, the soul is the formal cause of an organism, as well as the efficient cause of its movement. However, *it is also the final cause of the organism*, for the whole organism tends toward the perfection of its nature as its end. A

---

[24] Aristotle, *Metaphysics*, H, 1044a 36 - b11.

horse attains its end or purpose, not when it serves its human master, but when it grows to maturity and attains the perfection of its own form. Therefore, the ordering of all things to some Being outside the world is foreign to the thought of Aristotle. For him, finality in the universe is *immanent* in things, for the final causes of movement are identical to the forms of the things themselves.

Saint Thomas does not share this view. Better still, he "improves" this view. For him, the material and formal causes of a thing are intrinsic to it, while the efficient and final causes are always extrinsic. The soul is the formal cause of the organism and the secondary efficient cause of its operations. He says that the soul is the "secondary" efficient cause of its operations because the operation of the soul always requires the *concurrence* of an extrinsic cause, which is God. With regard to finality, Saint Thomas insists that creatures do not exist for themselves alone but for God. For everything tends to manifest the glory of the Creator. Therefore, God Himself must be the end or final cause of all things.

Saint Thomas' concept of God is far from being a copy of the Aristotelian God. Although Saint Thomas only borrowed from Aristotle the concept of God as First Unmoved Mover, still Saint Thomas' God is not the same as Aristotle's First Mover. What is the difference?

For Aristotle, the First Mover is a *final cause*, not an efficient cause. It is, indeed, the first cause of motion in the world, but it moves the universe, not by efficient physical causation, but by attraction. It draws the whole world into itself as an object of desire. The First Mover moves the heavenly spheres by inspiring love, which is why Aristotle had to postulate the presence of Intelligences in the celestial spheres. Also, Aristotle's First Mover is only a cause of movement, not a cause of being. The world is already there, eternal, and needing no God to create it. Therefore, the Aristotelian First Mover is not a creator, but solely and simply a First Mover.

In his *Metaphysics* Aristotle argues that this moving, but Unmoved Principle must be a pure act, without any potentiality whatsoever and, therefore, immaterial (since materiality implies a potentiality for change). Being immaterial, the First Mover cannot perform bodily action, but only spiritual and purely intellectual action. So, if God is the First Mover, then God must be active, and His activity must be one of Thought, not of physical exercise. What is the object of His thought? Aristotle thinks that the answer must be God Himself, for the object of God's knowledge must be the best of all possible objects.

The Aristotelian God is a subsistent Thought, the "Thought of Thought."[25] But this God thinks only of Himself, not of the world. Therefore, Aristotle's God as First Mover is not a providential God. It has no thought of the world or man. It is futile for man to try to establish a personal relationship with this God, for the God of Aristotle cannot be an object of worship, prayer or adoration. Although this God does not refuse to be loved, He in turn does not return our love. Between man and the Aristotelian God there can be no friendship.

Is this the thought of Saint Thomas? Far from it. The God of Saint Thomas is, indeed, a First Unmoved Mover, but He moves not merely as a final cause, but as an *efficient cause*. He is not merely a cause of becoming, but a cause of being, a Creator-God. On the word of God, Saint Thomas believes that the world was created. Guided by this faith, he discovered the philosophical *reasons* why the world was not necessarily eternal.

Like the Aristotelian God, the God of Saint Thomas is an *actus purus*, an active God, a thinking God. But unlike the Aristotelian God, the God of Saint Thomas is not a selfish God. The true God thinks of the world and man. He is not merely a fatherly God, but a friendly God, one who seeks and reciprocates human love. God created man for Himself, but *not for His sake but for man's sake*.

---

[25] See Aristotle, *Metaphysics*, 1074b 31-8.

Saint Thomas' and Aristotle's disparate opinions on the nature of God naturally have important consequences on their views on ethics. Although both of them regard happiness as the ultimate subjective end of man, Aristotle thinks that the happiness of man consists solely in a life of natural contemplation and practical wisdom. This is because Aristotle could not find an objective reality, not even in his First Mover, that could satisfy man's desire for happiness.

On the other hand, Saint Thomas agrees with Aristotle that man cannot find the object of his happiness in anything of this world. No creature can make him perfectly happy. Neither wealth, nor honor, nor fame nor the love of friends can make him perfectly happy. Not even the vision of an angel can make man perfectly happy because human desire is as infinite as the human mind can conceive. However, Saint Thomas knows from revelation that God has predestined man for the beatific vision of His Essence, in which there is eternal delight. "The eye has not seen, O God," the prophet says, "what things You have prepared for those who wait for You" (Isaiah 64:4). So, Saint Thomas knows that there is an objective reality that can satisfy the human heart. It is not vain to seek eternal happiness in an infinite good, for God has promised Himself to us.

Strictly speaking, even Saint Thomas could not have conceived of the joyful contemplation of the Divine Essence as man's objective beatitude, had not God Himself revealed this fact to us. God is so transcendent and so infinite as not to be a naturally attainable object of desire. Of course, man in his purely natural state could still desire to see God. But it will be, as in Aristotle, a *conditional* and *inefficacious desire*: "I wish I could see God face to face, if only it were possible." A true participation in the life of God is possible only with the aid of God Himself. But reason alone can neither prove nor disprove the possibility of that gratuitous gift — the "light of glory" — by which man can see and enjoy the infinite plenitude of Divine Being.

If Saint Thomas knew that there exists an objective reality that could satisfy the infinite cravings of the human heart, it is not because he was able to prove this philosophically. Rather, it is because he believed God's word for it. He got the correct answer concerning the true meaning of human existence because he humbly sought the guidance of divine revelation. Faith perfected his reason as grace perfects nature.

Now we see why, even in a philosophical effort to understand reality, the guidance of divine revelation must be sought. A purely natural metaphysics *is* possible, but it will be, as in Aristotle, a metaphysics where God is merely an object of speculation, but not the cause of eternal delight. A purely human ethics *is* possible. But it will be, as in Aristotle, an ethics for a possible man, not an ethics for the actual human being in his present condition as a fallen, but redeemed creature. This is why a philosophy that does not seek the guidance of revelation will fall, "and fall again."[26] After hearing the Christian revelation, philosophy may no longer proceed as if God never revealed Himself to humankind. The God of the philosophers is no longer, as the worldly wise still see Him, the Aristotelian First Mover — unconcerned and unreachable. Philosophy *must* be Christian if it is to be true, and it must see the First Mover as Saint Thomas saw Him — as a personal and providential Father, Creator of the World and the God of Abraham, Isaac and Jacob. Any attempt now to keep philosophy purely "natural" will be nothing less than a betrayal of wisdom.

---

[26] See Etienne Gilson, *The Spirit of Medieval Philosophy* (New York: Charles Scribner's Sons, 1940), p. 5.

Chapter Five

Saint Thomas and Philosophy

To extol a medieval theologian like Saint Thomas Aquinas might seem odd in an age like ours. But justice and a sense of gratitude oblige us to give credit to a man who, in the words of Pope John XXII, "enlightened the Church more than all the other doctors together."[1] If we singled out Saint Thomas among the thousands of thinkers who could be called "philosophers," it is because he offered us a perennial philosophy. His philosophy is alive, profound, lucid and open to faith. Maybe Saint Thomas today has few adherents and his intellectual opponents are many. But what does that matter? Long ago Heraclitus said, "Thousands of learned men do not counterbalance one single excellent master."[2]

Saint Thomas gave us, both in his writings and in his life, an example of how a man should dispose himself in the search for truth. The first requirement, he told us, was that learners should be *humble,*[3] for "where humility is, there also is wisdom" (Proverbs 11:2). The humble man recognizes that he does not have a monopoly on truth, and that others before him also have something

---

[1] John XXII, *Consistorial Address*, 1318.

[2] Heraclitus, *Fragments, 113*. Pope John XXII in the same address (1318) says of Saint Thomas: "A man can derive more profit from his books in one year than from a lifetime spent in pondering the philosophy of others."

[3] See Saint Thomas' inaugural lecture as Professor in the University of Paris.

to offer in the way to wisdom. Therefore, the humble man does not disregard earlier thinkers. He respects them and listens to their views. It is for this reason that Saint Thomas honored Aristotle with the title "philosopher *par excellence*," for Aristotle always reviewed the opinions of his predecessors before presenting his own.[4] Saint Thomas emulated this very well. So, Cajetan also said of him, "Because he had the utmost reverence for the Doctors of antiquity, he seems to have inherited in a way the intellect of all."[5]

In praising Saint Thomas Aquinas we do not intend to praise a medieval philosophy. If the philosophy of Saint Thomas is precious, it is not because it is medieval but because it is perennial. If it has stood the test of time, it is not because it is popular but because it is true. The Christian philosophy of Saint Thomas is clear, which is not to say that it is easy. In truth, understanding Saint Thomas is very difficult because his thought is imbued with a *realism* that makes it as complicated as the reality that it attempts to explain. In contrast, modern philosophers are simplistic rather than realistic. The Idealists simplified cosmology by reducing the world to an Idea. The Determinists simplified psychology by doing away with human freedom. The Relativists simplified epistemology by reducing all truth to "one's point of view."

There is a penalty for these all too simple explanations of the philosophers. *They fail the empirical test*. They contradict the facts of common experience. Samuel Johnson refuted Berkeley's Idealist philosophy by kicking a large stone. Chesterton embarrassed the Determinist by asking him why he says "Thank you" for the mustard. The English philosopher Henry More answered the Relativist — who said that it did not really matter whether you say

---

[4] In his book *On the Soul*, Book I, Chapter 2, 403b 20, Aristotle said that it is necessary "to call into council the views of those of our predecessors... in order that we may profit by whatever is sound in their suggestions and avoid their errors." Tr. by Richard McKeon in *The Basic Works of Aristotle*, p. 538.

[5] Cajetan, *Commentary on the Summa*, II-II, Q. 148, a. 4, toward the end.

that an object is moving toward you, or you are moving toward the object[6] — by asking why he got tired after running to his destination.[7]

Saint Thomas' philosophy is very difficult, but it squares with common experience. He thought that the world was a reality and not a dream. This is better than the philosophy of Berkeley who thought that the world was only an idea. Saint Thomas taught that man was a free being, destined by God for eternal happiness, unlike some philosophers who spent their life with the sole purpose of proving that life was purposeless. Saint Thomas thought that things were absolute but dependent on God, unlike the Relativist who regarded everything as relative, but not to anything absolute. Saint Thomas adored God as a personal Spirit who takes care of us, unlike Ernst Haeckel who derisively called God a "gaseous invertebrate." In other words, the doctrines of Saint Thomas are in accord with common understanding. This is the reason for their universal appeal.

THE LANGUAGE OF THOMISTIC PHILOSOPHY

Modern critics often denounce the followers of Saint Thomas for using a medieval language that, they say, is now meaningful only to a handful of monks and theologians. These critics say that terms taken from ancient and medieval philosophy, such as "potency" and "act," or "matter" and "form," are passé. They do not mean anything to modern man anymore, and they only make philosophical literature dry reading. Like the fourteenth century critics of scholasticism, these critics say that contemporary philosophers should refrain from using not only the terminology, but even the methodology of medieval theologians. They say that definitions and

---

[6] This is Descartes' thesis on the relativity of movement.
[7] Henry More, Letter of March 5, 1649.

distinctions, which they deride as useless "hair-splitting," should be avoided in philosophical expositions or treatises.

It is true that a philosopher, who wants to communicate a message effectively, must express his thoughts in a language that is understandable and meaningful to his contemporaries. However, it is incorrect to think that a language is no longer meaningful just because it employs ancient terms. Often, this manner of thinking is the result of bias, not against vocabulary, but against medieval philosophy. We never hear a mathematician criticized for using the Latin word *locus*, but a Thomist invites instant criticism when he uses a word such as *habitus*. Everyone listens respectfully to a doctor who says, "I will perform a *frontal lobotomy*," but a Thomist will probably receive an unpleasant frown if he starts his argument with, "Let me first distinguish the *major*." What is wrong with a technical language for philosophy? Even the physical and biological sciences cannot dispense with a special vocabulary, often more artificial than that of medieval philosophy. Phrases like "moment of inertia" or "logarithmic functions of a complex variable" are unfamiliar to almost everyone, except to engineers, scientists and mathematicians. If philosophy is a science — and indeed it is the Ruler of the Sciences — then it also has a right to its own technical jargon. Modern critics who are overwhelmed by the technical precision of the scholastic language should understand that the precise terms used by Saint Thomas and other scholastic philosophers serve to manifest truths rather than conceal them.

The fact that ancient terms make philosophy very difficult reading is not a very convincing reason for avoiding them. Contemporary writers who avoid ancient terms are not easier to read just because their terms are new. Is Heidegger's description of man as "ontic-ontological" easier to understand than the Aristotelian definition of man as a "rational animal"? Consider also some passages from Jean-Paul Sartre's *L'Etre et le Néant* as he distinguished the being-in-itself (*l'en-soi*) from the being-for-itself (*le pour soi*):

"Being is. Being is in-itself. Being is what it is."
"The For-itself, in fact, is nothing but the pure nihilation of
     the In-itself."
"Yet the For-itself *is*. It *is*, we may say, even if it is a being
which is not what it is and which is what it is not."[8]

Is this easier reading? Yet it involves no old-fashioned terms
like "potency" and "act." The difficulty in reading Saint Thomas
arises from a lack of familiarity with the vocabulary. The difficulty
in reading a philosopher like Sartre arises from the lack of coherent
meaning itself. A statement, such as, "the For-itself is a being which
is not what it is and which is what it is not," is, to say the least, very
confusing. Perhaps Sartre was not really denying the principle of
non-contradiction. Since he opposed the For-itself with the In-itself
as the latter's negation, then if the In-itself is "what it is," it follows
that the For-itself is "a being which is not what it (In-itself) is, and
which is what it (In-itself) is not." However, Sartre was unclear
because without any warning he shifted the denotation of the
pronoun "It," which grammatically refers only to the For-itself, to
refer to the In-itself. This is not just a new way of saying things. Since
Sartre mixed up the meaning of words, he really said nothing.

The language of Saint Thomas may lack the literary appeal of
Kahlil Gibran, but that is because his arguments speak to reason
rather than to the emotions. Clarity and logic are the requirements
of intellectual communication. No wonder then that the older liturgy
for his feast day describes his language as "brief in style, pleasing,
lofty, firm and clear in content."[9] This is the reason why adopting
the language of Saint Thomas makes sense in the modern world.
We live at a time when language is often abused so as no longer to
serve its purpose of evincing the "splendor of truth." In the words

---

[8] Quotations are from Hazel E. Barnes' translation, *Being and Nothingness* (New
   York: Philosophical Library, 1956), pp. lxvi, 617 and 79.

[9] II Nocturne, IV Responsory. Regrettably, the prayer is no longer in the current
   Liturgy of the Hours.

of Johnny Martin, "Language is a wonderful thing. It can be used to express our thoughts, to conceal our thoughts, or to *replace* thinking." The abuses in language so rampant in our day, and the too frequent appeal to poetry as a substitute for logic, is an indication of the world's metaphysical poverty. It is the regrettable consequence of the world's unfair prejudice against the terminology and methodology of scholastic philosophy.

THE BRANCHES OF PHILOSOPHY IN THE TRADITION OF SAINT THOMAS

In the philosophy of Saint Thomas the scope of philosophy is the whole contingent reality. However, the followers of Saint Thomas divide the field of philosophy into several parts, each possessing its formal unity. They do this to make the presentation of philosophy more orderly. Also, it makes the learning of philosophy easier, especially for beginners. The various branches of philosophy in the Thomistic tradition are as follows.

    I   Systematic Philosophy: Basic Disciplines
        A. Speculative Philosophy
           1. Philosophy of Nature
             a) Cosmology
             b) Psychology
           2. Metaphysics
             a) Ontology
             b) Theodicy
             c) Critique
           3. Logic
        B. Practical Philosophy
           1. Philosophy of Art
           2. Moral Philosophy
             a) Ethics
             b) Social Philosophy

II Systematic Philosophy: Special Disciplines
    A. Philosophy of Science
    B. Philosophy of Mathematics
    C. Philosophy of Education
    D. Philosophy of History

III History of Philosophy
    A. Ancient Philosophy
    B. Medieval Philosophy
    C. Modern and Current Philosophy

Systematic Philosophy

The major division of philosophy is that between *systematic philosophy* and *history of philosophy*. Systematic philosophy gives an orderly exposition of philosophical principles, conclusions and opinions, while the history of philosophy gives a chronological account of the development of philosophical ideas and their significant relations. Systematic philosophy is so called, *not* because it presents philosophy as a deductive system a là Spinoza or Hegel, but simply because it presents philosophical truths in a coherent and orderly fashion. As the history of philosophy shows, a genuine philosophical edifice is not built in the way that Euclid's *Elements* were built, that is, by a one-man deduction from a set of "unchallengeable" propositions. Rather, philosophy results from the collaborative effort of various thinkers who labor to discover truth from principles embedded in *common* experience. Systematic philosophy does not "demonstrate" philosophical truths after the manner of mathematics, but after the manner of an *empirical* science. Using self-evident principles common to all the sciences, systematic philosophy analyzes the data of common experience by an inductive-deductive approach. It formulates and gathers opinions and hypotheses, puts competing theories to the test and, where verification in common experience is not possible, it checks them at least for internal consistency.

The *basic disciplines* of systematic philosophy constitute the core of the *philosophia perennis*. Its branches are *speculative philosophy* and *practical philosophy*. Speculative philosophy deals with beings to the extent that they are *knowable*, while practical philosophy deals with beings to the extent that they are operable (or capable of being made or done). The use of the word "speculative" is misleading because this part of philosophy does not consist of speculations, but of truths and probable opinions verified in common experience. The word "speculative" here does not mean "conjecture." Rather, it has the same meaning as the Latin verb *speculor*, which means, "to see, to inspect, to examine or to explore." Speculative philosophy deals with beings, not to the extent that they could be made or done, but to the extent that they could be "seen, inspected, investigated or explored" by the mind. On the other hand, practical philosophy (from the Greek *praxis*, which means action) is not speculative but *normative*. It seeks knowledge, not of facts, but of the rules for action, either in the making of beautiful or useful artifacts, or in the performance of good human acts.

The parts of speculative philosophy are the *philosophy of nature* and *metaphysics*. The philosophy of nature deals with a particular kind of being, namely, bodily being. On the other hand, metaphysics deals with beings *as beings*. It deals with beings (not necessarily bodily) to the extent that they are beings. It might seem more logical to treat metaphysics, which deals with beings in general, before the philosophy of nature, which deals with a particular kind of being. For pedagogical reasons, however, the presentation of philosophy usually begins with the philosophy of nature because its object is more familiar to us.

Cosmology is that part of the philosophy of nature which deals with the bodily world, or the world of mobile beings. On the other hand, *psychology* deals with mobile beings that have life. Do not confuse these two sciences with the corresponding experimental sciences bearing the same names of "cosmology" and "psychology." The latter sciences deal only with the observable and measurable aspects of mobile beings, and stop short of first causes.

Ontology deals with beings in general. *Theodicy* (or, more properly, natural theology) deals with God as the First Cause of contingent being. *Critique* (which is different from what the ancients called "material logic") deals with real beings as they relate to the knowing mind.

Logic is the science and art of sound thinking. As an *art*, logic is not itself a part of philosophy or of any other science in particular, for it is the instrument of reason itself in its quest for truth. Students endeavor to acquire first the art of logic (in conjunction with grammar and rhetoric) before engaging in any scientific endeavor because it is the common instrument of the sciences. For this reason, the ancient masters call the art of logic a *propædeutic* to the sciences. As *science*, however, logic is a part of philosophy that deals with "second intentions." These are the properties that beings have in the mind, not as objects in reality ("first intentions"), but as objects of thought. Since second intentions follow the first intentions and proceed from them, so logic, as science, is placed after the sciences of real beings.

Operable objects, which are the proper objects of practical philosophy, are of two kinds. They are either actions involved (a) in the *making* of things or (b) in the *doing* of human acts. The consideration of the rules that regulate the acts of making things (artifacts) belongs to the *philosophy of art*. Its object is in the sphere of *production*. The study of the norms that regulate the doing of properly human acts belongs to *moral philosophy*. Its object is in the sphere of human *action*. The branches of moral philosophy are *ethics*, which deals with human acts pertaining to man as an individual, and *social philosophy*, which deals with human acts pertaining to man as a member of society.

The special disciplines of speculative philosophy contain

extended treatment of certain subjects that properly belong to one or more of the basic disciplines. For example, the topics discussed in the *philosophy of science* and the *philosophy of mathematics* partly belong to metaphysics, and partly to the philosophy of nature. On the other hand, the *philosophy of education* and the *philosophy of history* both belong partly to psychology and partly to social philosophy. The list of special disciplines given in the schema is not exhaustive. One may add other disciplines to the list, such as the philosophy of labor, the philosophy of criticism, etc.

History of Philosophy as Part of Philosophy

Although not formally a part of philosophy, a study of the *history of philosophy* is a pre-requisite in understanding the philosophical tradition of Saint Thomas. Some scholars have the mistaken opinion that the history of philosophy consists merely in recording the thoughts of past philosophers. If this is so, then the result would be a history of their philosophies, not a history of philosophy. Of course, philosophical thoughts come from philosophers, but philosophy itself is independent of philosophers.[10] As Saint Thomas said, "The study of philosophy is that we may know not what men have taught but what the truth of things is."[11] Therefore, the history of philosophy is the history of ideas and their relations, irrespective of who conceived the idea first, or when, how or why it was so conceived. Viewed in this manner, the history of

---

[10] Etienne Gilson, *The Unity of Philosophical Experience* (New York: Charles Scribner's Sons, 1937), Part IV, Ch. 12, p. 302: "It seems, therefore, that though philosophical ideas can never be found separate from philosophers and their philosophies, they are, to some extent, independent of philosophers as well as of their philosophies. Philosophy consists in the concepts of philosophers, taken in the naked, impersonal necessity of both their contents and their relations. The history of these concepts and of their relationships is the history of philosophy itself."

[11] Saint Thomas Aquinas, *On the Heavens* (*In Libros de Coelo et Mundo Expositio*), I, Lesson 22.

philosophy may more readily be regarded as part of philosophy than the history of science is part of science. Etienne Gilson said, "It is not impossible to become a competent scientist without knowing much about the history of science, but no man can carry very far his own philosophical reflections unless he first studies the history of philosophy."[12]

There are three principal periods in the development of Western philosophy. The first is that of Ancient Philosophy, which saw the triumph of human reason in the discourses of the Greeks. Next is the age of Medieval Philosophy, which witnessed the illumination of reason by faith in the Christian revelation. The third is the present age of Modern and Current Philosophy, which has been marked since the Renaissance by the rise of rationalism and the ascendancy of science.

---

[12] Etienne Gilson, *The Unity of Philosophical Experience*, Foreword, p. vii.

Chapter Six

The Future of Philosophy

Strictly speaking, philosophy is for everyone because it represents the common conversation of humankind concerning essential questions that people have raised and attempted to answer through the ages. What is man? What is his destiny? Is there life after death? Is there a God? These are a few of the questions that intrigue people everywhere. In this sense philosophy is not the monopoly of professional philosophers. It is the concern of every thinking human being, whether he be a politician, a scientist, a poet, or a peasant.

Francis Bacon was a statesman, John Locke a medical doctor, Baruch Spinoza a lens grinder, but they all engaged in philosophy. Man does not philosophize because he is a doctor, or because he is a craftsman, or even because he is a professional philosopher, but solely and simply because he is human. Philosophy is for everyone because even the enemies of philosophy philosophize when they say that philosophy is impossible.[1]

---

[1] Aristotle advanced the following dilemma in a fragment of one of his lost treatises, *Protreptikos*, Fragment 50, 1483b 29; 1484a 2, 8, 18: "You say one must philosophize. Then you must philosophize. You say one should not philosophize. Then to prove your contention you must philosophize. In any case one must philosophize." Quoted from Nicholas Horvath, *Philosophy* (Barron's Educational Series, 1974), p. 3. A similar rendering is in E.I. Watkin's translation of Jacques Maritain's *Introduction to Philosophy* (New York: Sheed & Ward), p. 104.

Saying that philosophy is for everyone does not mean that everybody is obliged to make philosophy his *profession*. Similarly, not everyone is obliged to be a medical doctor, although we say that everyone should be concerned about his health. Often, people cannot live on philosophy alone. Happy are they who have been blessed by good fortune to make a living successfully while in pursuit of wisdom.

On the other hand, in saying that not everybody is obliged to be a professional philosopher, we do not mean that people need to pursue wisdom only superficially. On the contrary, triviality and mediocrity have no place in philosophy. Since philosophy aims at wisdom, its achievement requires discipline, proficiency, and a high degree of precision on the part of the thinker. As an intellectual enterprise, wisdom requires that it be pursued assiduously. In this respect philosophy differs from other intellectual enterprises. Mortimer Adler noted that we don't need to be skilled in the arts and sciences to be human, but we all need as much philosophical knowledge and sagacity as our capacity will allow to live a fully human life. This is true, whether we are called to be professional philosophers or not.

If philosophy is for everyone, then why are there only few who engage in it? There are three reasons.

First, philosophy is not a productive science or, as William James puts it, philosophy "bakes no bread." This fact makes it distasteful to those whose minds are focused on worldly pursuits. Colleges today offer less philosophical subjects in their curricula than productive courses, for the aims of philosophy do not conform with those of worldly pursuits. As Joseph Pieper said, to philosophize is, in a way, "to step out of this workaday world." Often, people will ridicule the philosopher because they find his ambitions foolish. When Thales of Miletus fell into a ditch while gazing at the stars, the handmaid of Thrace laughed at him.[2] She said that the

---

[2] Plato, *Theaetetus*, 174A.

philosopher was so enterprising to know what was going on in heaven, that he failed to notice what was before his feet. Her laughter reflects the attitude of this pragmatic world to the seeming uselessness of philosophy. The philosopher has always been an occasion of laughter because "... as he forgets earthly interests and is rapt in the divine, the vulgar deem him mad, and rebuke him; they do not know that he is inspired."[3]

Second, the intellectual discipline demanded by philosophy is very difficult, and there are only few who are willing to take it. As Bertrand Russell aptly remarks, "Many men would sooner die than think. In fact they do." The choice to be a philosopher is something that very few would make, for it implies, Immanuel Kant noted, abandoning an easy life for a life of virtue.[4] It is a choice between a life of sacrifice and a life of sensible pleasure, a choice between great learning and material success, between wisdom and mediocrity. In the words of Epictetus, it is a choice either "to be a philosopher or one of the mob."[5]

Third, the disagreement among philosophers scandalizes many people. The world is full of thinking but there is no agreement in thought. There are many philosophers, but they have no common philosophy. On the one hand, there are scholars who glorify science. On the other hand, there are professors who discredit human reason. In the midst of this intellectual turmoil, people do not find enough Masters to guide them along the pathways of wisdom, and who rise to defend the dignity of human reason against the onslaughts of irrationalism. Unless the warriors of truth put on their armor to fight the rivals of wisdom, there is no

---

[3] Socrates, as quoted by Plato in the *Phaedrus*, 249B. Tr. by Benjamin Jowett in *The Dialogues of Plato*, Vol. 7 of *Great Books* (Encyclopædia Britannica, Inc., 1952), p. 126.

[4] Immanuel Kant, *Critique of Practical Reason*, Part I, II, 1.

[5] Epictetus, *Encheiridion*, XXIX. This quotation is from Mortimer Adler and Charles Van Doren's *Great Treasury of Western Thought*, p. 1092.

hope of struggling successfully against this tide of confusion and despair. This is the crisis that philosophy faces today: *we lack warriors to fight for wisdom.*

Now we see what becoming a philosopher means today. It is not merely the call to carry on the perennial conversation in the face of present difficulties. It is also the call to sacrifice pleasure and material success for the sake of wisdom. It is the call to be a warrior, to defend philosophy against the charge of bankruptcy, and to regain for the world a sense of, and esteem for, contemplation.

Some people say that the attempt to revive philosophy is futile, for philosophy has reached the end of the road. They advise us to abandon the pursuit of wisdom altogether and give up the fight against the enemies of wisdom. We must resist this cowardly counsel. As Nietzsche says, wisdom requires courage: "Courageous, untroubled, mocking, violent — that is what wisdom wants us to be: wisdom is a woman and loves only a warrior."[6]

THE FUTURE OF PHILOSOPHY

In his book, *The Pleasures of Philosophy*, Will Durant wrote of how the people once valued and esteemed "Lady Wisdom" (philosophy) more highly than a kingdom:

> Once the strongest men were willing to die for her: Socrates chose to be her martyr rather than live in flight before her enemies; Plato risked himself twice to win a kingdom for her; Marcus Aurelius loved her more passionately than his throne; and Bruno burned at the stake for loyalty to her. Once thrones and papacies feared philosophy and imprisoned her votaries lest dynasties should fall. Athens exiled Protagoras, and Alexandria trembled be-

---

[6] Friedrich Nietzsche, *Thus Spoke Zarathustra*, Part I, "Of Reading and Writing," Tr. by R.J. Hollingdale in *A Nietzsche Reader* (Penguin Books, 1977), p. 17.

fore Hypatia; a great pope courted timidly the friendship of Erasmus; regents and kings hounded Voltaire from their lands, and fretted in jealousy when at last all the civilized world bowed before the sceptre of his pen. Dionysius and Dionysius' son offered Plato the mastery of Syracuse; Alexander's royal aid made Aristotle the most learned man in history; a scholar-king lifted Francis Bacon almost to the leadership of England, and protected him from his enemies; and the great Frederick, at midnight when all his pompous generals had gone to sleep, held high revelry with poets and philosophers, envious of their boundless realms and their timeless sway.[7]

Such has been philosophy's glorious past. Philosophy today has a different status. It has lost the respectability that it once had. science and technology took its place in the great universities. The present condition of philosophy is so bad that Mortimer J. Adler said that he would not advise a young man to take up a career in philosophy today. "I do not think," he said, "that it (philosophy) is an enterprise he can look forward to engaging without misgivings, without apologies, and with complete self-respect and satisfaction."[8]

Why do people no longer pursue wisdom today? Why do they not give philosophy the same respect they give to modern science? Historians of philosophy put the blame on philosophers themselves. For example, Will Durant complained that philosophers have put more effort in answering trivial epistemological questions than in answering essential questions about the world and man. Philosophers of the last two centuries have argued endlessly about

---

[7] Will Durant, *The Pleasures of Philosophy* (New York: Simon & Schuster, 1953), p. 1. COPYRIGHT © 1953, 1981 by Will Durant. Reprinted by permission of Simon & Schuster, Inc.

[8] Mortimer J. Adler, *The Conditions of Philosophy* (New York: Atheneum, 1965), Part 1, Ch. 1, n. 2, p. 6.

whether the world really existed, and whether they had a mind to know it.

> And as philosophy has been written these last two hundred years, it may well deserve this dishonor and oblivion. What has philosophy been since Bacon and Spinoza died? For the most part it has been epistemology, the scholastic theology of knowledge, the technical and esoteric, the mystic and incomprehensible dispute about the existence of the external world. The intelligence that might have made philosopher-kings has gone to erudite analyses of the reasons for and against the possibility that stars and oceans and bacteria and neighbors exist when they are not perceived. And for two hundred and fifty years this battle of the frogs and mice has been going on, with no appreciable result for philosophy or life, and with no profit for any man but the printer.[9]

Gilbert Keith Chesterton had written similar observations. He said that philosophy lost its popularity because modern philosophers have abandoned common sense in pursuit of the mystifying and the trivial.

> Since the modern world began in the sixteenth century, nobody's system of philosophy has really corresponded to everybody's sense of reality; to what, if left to themselves, common men would call common sense. Each started with a paradox; a peculiar point of view demanding the sacrifice of what they would call a sane point of view. That is the one thing common to Hobbes and Hegel, to Kant and Bergson, to Berkeley and William James. A man had to believe something that no normal man would believe, if it were suddenly propounded to his simplicity; as that law is above right, or right is outside reason, or things are only

---

[9] Will Durant, *op. cit.*, pp. 2-3.

as we think them, or everything is relative to a reality that is not there.[10]

When philosophers indulge in the esoteric and the trivial, philosophy loses its attraction to ordinary people. So, if philosophy seems to have reached the end of the road, it is because modern philosophers have betrayed philosophy.

Mortimer J. Adler explains that the problem with philosophy today is not that it has reached the end of the road. The real problem is that it is on the *wrong* road. Modern philosophers are not dealing with the right questions. In his book, *The Conditions of Philosophy*, he states that philosophy must deal primarily with "first-order questions." This means that philosophy must deal chiefly with questions about the world and man, and less with "second-order questions," which are not about the world, but about *our minds* and *how we know* the world.[11] In stating this condition, he opposed many contemporary philosophers who, like the Idealists of the last three centuries, have regarded the problems of philosophy to consist mainly of epistemological questions.

Mr. Adler adds that philosophy must be in harmony with common sense to be respectable.[12] In stating this condition he also opposed modern phenomenologists whose doctrines have been esoteric, and whose methods of analysis make little or no sense to the average person. He chided the existentialist philosophers, namely, Kierkegaard, Heidegger, Jaspers, Sartre, Merleau-Ponty and Marcel. For, although concerned with "first-order questions" about human life and existence, they conduct philosophy, not as a common conversation of minds, but as a purely private affair.

What then is the future of philosophy? It is hard to say. Many

---

[10] Gilbert Keith Chesterton, *St. Thomas Aquinas: "The Dumb Ox"* (Garden City, NY: Image Books, 1956), Ch. 6, p. 145.

[11] Mortimer J. Adler, *op. cit.*, Ch. 2, n. 5.

[12] Mortimer J. Adler, *op. cit.*, Ch. 3, n. 3.

people today embrace various forms of eastern philosophy. This indicates contemporary man's unquenchable thirst for a knowledge beyond science. Unfortunately, the eastern philosophical schools do not significantly help to restore the respectability of philosophy. Their doctrines equally range from the enigmatic to the absurd. If the analytico-linguistic, phenomenological, existentialist and eastern philosophical movements continue to dominate philosophical thinking in the years ahead, then philosophy will continue to have a bleak future. However, if enough philosophers wage a war against the counterfeits of wisdom, then, as Mortimer Adler also said, philosophy *can* have a future that is even brighter than its past. Ultimately the future of philosophy depends, not so much on the acuteness of our minds, but on the grace of God and the good will of contemporary man.